THE LEICAFLEX BOOK

THEO KISSELBACH

THE LEICAFLEX BOOK

Translated from the German by
F. Bradley, A. I. I. P., A. R. P. S.

Second Edition

HEERING-VERLAG
SEEBRUCK AM CHIEMSEE
1972

Title of the Original German Edition:

DAS LEICAFLEX-BUCH

Printed in West Germany
© 1969/1972 Heering-Verlag GmbH, Seebruck am Chiemsee (West Germany). Only authorized
translation. All rights including that of reproduction in whole or in part expressly reserved.
Printed by Heering-Verlag GmbH, Munich 25
ISBN 3 7763 3281 6

PREFACE

The Leicaflex is a single-lens reflex camera of high precision. Many photographers have been waiting for it for many years. This book has been written to show, in theory and practice, its performance and achievements and how it is handled. This revised edition includes everything you need to know about the Leicaflex SL and about the many new accessories, which enlarge its system considerably.

It is the object of technology to make operations easier, not to tie us down to slavish performance; the Leicaflex is therefore not fully automatic, operating according to a firmly laid down scheme. You have retained complete freedom of action. It is, after all, not very difficult to decide whether it is the shutter speed or the lens stop that should play the more important part during an exposure. Your creative latitude is all the greater if you can employ all your photographic facilities of your own free choice.

Of all our sense organs the eye is the most active in photography. To serve it the Leicaflex has been equipped with a brilliant, bright viewfinder which allows you to survey the most important functions of your camera, and enables you to decide about the right moment of exposure.

The Leicaflex is a system camera, i. e. a number of ingeniously matched lenses of excellent correction enlarge your possibilities of pictorial reproduction and continuously stimulate your imagination in your photographic practice.

If you can play the violin, you will highly appreciate the ownership of a "Stradivarius". But nobody will expect such a magic instrument to play on its own. It reveals its whole performance and wonderful timbre only in response to the talent of a true artist. If you are a discriminating photographer, you will value the Leicaflex highly. But it will show its quality only when you, the owner, can handle it with the same virtuosity as the accomplished musician plays his instrument.

CONTENTS

THE CAMERA IN ACTION

The basic concepts of photography

For the author of a technical book the opening chapter is the most difficult to write. Where should he begin? Every reader should be familiar with some basic concepts; most readers are. But where can the beginner find help, can he be expected to buy another book and study it before he can hope to understand the present one? Hardly. It is therefore my business to present these concepts as lucidly and graphically as possible; to the advanced worker I would suggest that he begin on p. 14.

To photograph means "to draw with light". The lens of a photographic camera projects a portion of our surroundings on the light-sensitive emulsion. This lens is a complicated optical system: the image formed by a single lens would suffer from too many defects.

Focal length

A lens enables us to form a concentrated image of the sun on a piece of paper, setting the paper alight. The distance between lens and paper is called "focal length". At this distance a sharp image is formed of all objects which are infinitely far away (∞). The focal length of the lens is engraved in figures on the front mount after the letter "f" (Latin : focus).

For objects at a shorter distance the distance between lens and film plane must be longer than the focal length. The lens must be focused on the object distance. The extension of the lens (beyond the focal length) increases as the object — lens distance decreases.

Lens speed

The maximum aperture of the lens is also engraved on its front mount, denoting its "speed". The figure indicates the ratio of lens diameter to focal length. A lens speed of f/2 means that the focal length is twice the free diameter of the lens with its diaphragm fully open (full aperture).

Iris diaphragm

An iris diaphragm is built into the lens to enable the photographer to reduce the intensity of the light reaching the film. The diaphragm scale in common use today consists of the following steps (depending on the type of lens only

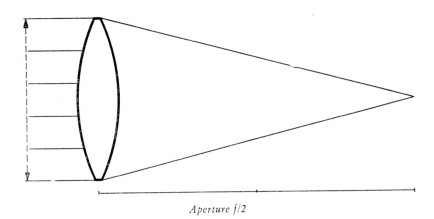

Aperture f/2

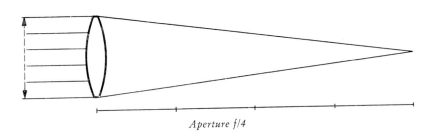

Aperture f/4

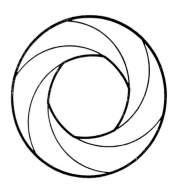

The diagrams show the relationship between diameter and focal length of the lens (the latter as a multiple of the former).

9

certain sections of the scale are used): 1 - 2.4 - 2 - 2.8 - 4 - 5.6 - 8 - 11 - 16-22 - 32. In the interest of simplicity "f/" is omitted, and only the figure engraved. Thus 4, for instance, means f/4. Since the aperture of the diaphragm constitutes an area, the quantity of light it transmits increases or decreases as the square of the diameter of the aperture. Accordingly, f/2 transmits four times as much light as f/4. For practical reasons the diaphragm values are graduated so that the next higher value on the diaphragm scale requires double the exposure time for the initial value. In the Leicaflex, values midway between the scale values can also be set.

The shutter

The quantity of light reaching the sensitive emulsion can also be controlled by means of the shutter. We distinguish between the between-lens shutter, built into the lens as its name implies, and the focal-plane shutter, in which a slit traversing the film at a close distance is responsible for the exposure. The Leicaflex has a very quick-acting focal-plane shutter that allows speeds of up to $1/2000$ second. Very high shutter speeds are indispensable if fast-moving objects are to appear sharp in the picture.

Depth of field

Strictly only those objects will appear sharp that are located at the distance on which the lens has been focused. Others, located in front of or behind the "focusing plane", will be unsharp. Every photographic image, however, has a certain 'depth of field', i.e. within a certain space in front of and behind the focusing plane the transition to unsharpness is not yet apparent. This region of sharpness decreases with the distance of the object focused (focusing distance). The depth of field depends also on the diaphragm aperture. The smaller this aperture, the greater the depth of field; very small apertures make it possible to reproduce objects at greatly varying distances (foreground and background) simultaneously sharp on the photograph. With large apertures and focus on objects in the near foreground the far background becomes so unsharp as to be quite immaterial to the context of the picture. The tolerance of unsharpness is expressed in mm in terms of the 'circle of confusion'; it has a diameter of $1/30$mm in the depth-of-field scales or tables for the 35mm format.

Explanation of the depth of field. The differences can be seen clearly in the four pictures of the model.

In the first picture the palm tree in the background was focused. Towards the foreground the contours become more and more blurred.

In the second picture the game hunter in the foreground was photographed at full aperture. Sharpness decreases rapidly towards the background.

In the third picture sharpness is in the plane of the warrior. Unsharpness in the fore- and background is reduced, but you will obtain really satisfactory sharpness throughout the whole range only if you reduce your lens aperture.

The focusing distance for the fourth picture therefore is identical with that in the third, but the lens was sufficiently stopped down. How far you can or should stop down depends on the photographic situation.

The depth-of-field scale on the lenses (p. 22) provides valuable information.

The photochemical process

The light-sensitive emulsion is 'exposed' in the camera. This exposure does not yet reveal a picture, which at this stage is said to be a 'latent image'. Although the picture exists, to be visible it must first be developed.

Development is a reduction process. Owing to a chemical reaction in the developer the silver bromide affected by light is split into its constituents of bromine and silver. The bromine enters the developer solution, the silver remains in the emulsion layer. The most important property of the developer is its power to blacken silver differentially, exactly corresponding to the degrees of brightness in the subject. These 'tone values' are, however, inverted, because blackening (a 'density') occurs only where the light was able to act. The unexposed silver bromide is removed in the fixing solution, to which the film is transferred after development. We now have a photographic negative, which after fixing must be washed and dried to ensure good keeping qualities. To obtain a positive picture from the negative in which the brightness gradation is similar to that of the original a sheet of light-sensitive paper must be exposed through the negative. The paper, too, is developed, fixed, washed, and dried. Basically, this is a repetition of the various stages of the negative process. Graduated densities appear on the paper, corresponding to the quantity of light it has received, and we obtain a negative of the original negative, i.e. a positive. By means of the positive process either contact prints, or, in an enlarger, enlarged positives can be produced.

A well-graded negative is essential to a good positive. After too short an exposure the negative is too transparent, containing too little detail in the shadow portions. Although it is well graded after too generous an exposure, it is denser than it need be. Whereas producing a positive from an underexposed negative may create difficulties, moderate overexposure does no harm unless there has been movement blur or camera shake. A certain amount of experience is required to anticipate and judge the effect of the future positive already in the negative. On festive occasions visitors to Rothenburg ob der Tauber are received by the burghers in tradional costumes. 90mm Elmarit f/2.8; f/8, 1/125sec.

THE SINGLE-LENS REFLEX CAMERA

Why single-lens? Are there also twin-lens cameras? Yes, indeed, but they are not stereo-cameras for three-dimensional pictures; they use a lens each, of the same focal length, for viewing and exposure. The single-lens type, on the other hand, uses the same lens for both procedures. The mirror, which makes the observation of the image possible, is only swung out of the optical path immediately before the exposure.

Since the taking lens decides the dimensions of the picture area also in its capacity as viewfinder lens, viewfinder field and picture field are always identical; this also applies to the close-up range and the use of long-focal-length lenses. In rangefinder and twin-lens reflex cameras the distance between the two optical systems may make itself felt (parallax). The time lag between shutter release and exposure is a little longer in the single-lens reflex camera than that in a rangefinder camera, because the mirror must first be swung out of the optical path. This does not exceed, however, about $1/30$ sec. During the last few years the single-lens reflex system has come to be regarded as particularly progressive.

First patented more than a century ago

But the method is not all that new, because the first patent concerned with it was applied for by Sutton as early as 1860. The large formats used in those days required an apparatus which was so bulky, heavy, and cumbersome to operate that the principle had only limited applications. After the turn of the century, when the 9 x 12cm format became popular, reflex cameras in this format, too, acquired a certain following. They were already equipped with a focal-plane shutter, and their technical refinement was considerable; but only a limited circle of enthusiasts could afford such expensive models.

Advance through the 35mm Leica format

Only after the Leica format, created by Oskar Barnack, had become generally accepted did the mirror-reflex principle attain its greatest popularity. The first cameras were already very practical, but their operation was still awkward, because the image had still to be observed via the mirror at an angle of 90°. In the horizontal format it was upright, but side-reversed. The vertical format was very inconvenient, because the image here was both upside-down and side-reversed.

'Pentaprism' — a magic word

The introduction of the pentaprism for viewing constituted the biggest advance in the development of the reflex camera. The pentaprism makes it possible to erect the image, which can now be viewed right-way-round and upright both in the horizontal and in the vertical position.

This does away with many limitations; a picture of moving subjects, previously difficult to take, has become as easy to obtain as with a rangefinder camera. The viewing direction, too, is no longer deflected through 90°, but has become parallel to the optical axis of the camera lens as in the rangefinder camera.

The hinged mirror almost without dark interval

The mirror movement, too, has been improved. In the early designs the mirror was swung out of the optical path shortly before the exposure, but did not return to its previous position. The viewfinder remained dark after the exposure until the shutter was rewound. Today the mirror returns immediately after the exposure (instant-return mirror) so that observation of the subject can be continued.

The brightness of the viewfinder image

For perfect observation the small 24 x 36mm format needs to be magnified 4–5 times. The entire viewfinder image can, however, be surveyed only if it incorporates, besides the magnifying system, an illuminating lens (field lens) that offers the eye sufficient brightness also in the marginal regions of the image. Often there is not enough space for a suitable field lens; the refractive power is then divided between a thinner lens and a Fresnel disc. The principle of transferring the refractive power of a lens to a stepped disc was discovered as early as 150 years ago by the French physicist Fresnel.

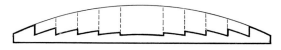

Only the first version of the Leicaflex includes a focusing disc with Fresnel steps; in the Leicaflex SL the base of the viewfinder prism is spherical, so that it functions as a collecting lens.

Groundglass screen, measuring wedge, micro-screen

The aerial image may be ideal for viewing, but it is unsuitable for focusing. The use of the groundglass screen for focusing the image in a single plane is therefore as old as photography itself. Groundglass screens differ a great deal in their finish and have textures of varying fineness. If it is too coarse, a groundglass screen diffuses the light very strongly, and fine detail can no longer be distinguished. If it is too fine the image is so transparent that it can no longer be observed with sufficient accuracy in the focusing plane. Eyes of particularly rapid accommodation, e. g. of young persons, will find focusing difficult.

Since the texture of groundglass screens various efforts have been made for years to find, if possible, more accurate focusing methods. Measuring wedges increase focusing accuracy, but their use is limited to certain narrow conditions. Corresponding to the wedge angle, the aperture of the lens must not fall below a certain value (e.g. f/5.6).

Conditions are similar with microprisms. These, however, have the advantage of being almost invisible after focusing, whereas the measuring wedge remains a disturbing feature in the centre of the image.

The fact that the image is observed at only about 4 x magnification creates a special difficulty. An eye of perfect acuity can resolve details of a minimum diameter of $1/40$mm in the plane of observation. Very good lenses, however, resolve far more than this. More than 30 % of persons not wearing spectacles do not enjoy full visual acuity and are therefore unable to focus with confidence. This defect can often be eliminated by means of correction lenses.

The automatic diaphragm

Focusing is more efficient at full than at a smaller aperture, because then the depth of field is at its shallowest. For viewing the subject full aperture is also more favourable because of the bright image it produces. Before lenses with automatic diaphragms were introduced, the lens had to be manually stopped down to the predetermined value before the exposure was made. The modern lenses with automatic diaphragm automatically control this function.

THE LEICAFLEX

The Leicaflex is a 35mm single-lens reflex camera of modern design with many valuable features. Its slightly curved back cannot escape your notice, it makes the camera slimmer and more stylish. It is hinged in order to speed up and facilitate insertion of the film.

The focal-plane shutter of the Leicaflex has special advantages. The time of travel of the shutter blinds is 10msec; this meets two requirements: it is now possible to synchronize electronic flash at $1/100$ sec; for the fastest movements $1/2000$ sec can be used, and without noticeable vibration at that.

Normally the two movements, that of the mirror and the shutter action, are coupled. Both functions are coordinated so that the shutter operates only after the mirror has left the optical path. This is achieved by means of a 'feeler' which the mirror strikes and immobilizes. The cushioning of the rapid mirror movements, too, is a masterpiece of precision engineering design. The mirror movement is impact-free, because a special gear mechanism brings it gently to a halt; it therefore causes practically no vibration.

The image is seen right-way-round and upright in a radiantly-bright viewfinder; it is focused by means of microprisms in the centre of the viewfinder, which is also the control centre for all adjustments. A number of lenses of various focal lengths are available for the Leicaflex; they can be changed by means of a bayonet mount, and include automatic diaphragms with feedback to the exposure meter. All exposure times, as well as the exposure meter itself, can also be read in the viewfinder.

The camera comes in two versions, which differ mainly in the principle of the exposure measurement. In the Leicaflex measurement is effected directly by a photo-resistor located below the prism on the front panel of the camera. In the Leicaflex SL the exposure is measured through the lens. The observation mirror is partly transparent, and via a second mirror a portion of the light is conducted through a photo-resistor near the base of the camera. Both systems allow free choice of lens aperture and shutter speed. Further details of these two systems will be described on the following pages:

Special features of the Leicaflex on pp. 27, of the Leicaflex SL pp. 44.

How does one hold the Leicaflex?

Whatever camera you use, the way you hold it and your technique of releasing the shutter have a decisive effect on the quality of your pictures. You can do justice to the optimum performance of the lens only with a flawless exposure technique. Slight camera shake is far more common than is generally realized.

Hold the Leicaflex as shown in the picture on the left. Grip the helical mount of the lens between your left thumb and index finger from below, thereby supporting the camera in its centre of gravity. Focus your subject and set the lens aperture in this position. During shutter release the left hand should not be moved. Hold the Leicaflex in your right hand so that your index finger rests on the release button, whereas the other fingers grip the housing. During shutter release, which should be smooth — all jerkiness should be avoided — the right hand supports the camera slightly. After the release the left hand supports the entire weight, so that the right hand is released and the thumb

18

can conveniently carry out the sweeping movement of the shutter winding lever.

The right-hand picture on p. 18 shows the position usual with most other cameras. It is inconvenient with the Leicaflex because it makes it necessary to change the position of the hands for both focusing and shutter winding.

For vertical pictures turn the camera so that the shutter winding lever faces upwards (picture on the left). Here, too, the lens is supported by the left hand. Press the camera body firmly to your head. It is more convenient to focus and to adjust lens aperture and shutter speed with the camera in the horizontal position and to turn it into the vertical position just before the moment of exposure. The alternative of turning the camera so that the shutter winding lever faces downwards (picture on the right) is inadvisable if you work without an ever-ready case because of the danger of accidentally pressing the rewind button (21), which may cause faulty film transport.

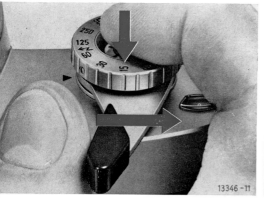 

Controls for the right hand

1. The *shutter winding lever* engages in two positions: parking (picture on
   the right), and readiness (picture on the left). After the shutter has been
   released the film is transported through the length of one frame; at the
   same time the shutter is wound, and the frame counter advanced to the
   next higher number. The shutter release mechanism is blocked if the winding lever has not been rotated as far as it will go. The lever will be easier
   to operate if the Leicaflex rests in the left hand.

2. The *release button* has an internal thread for the cable release. Pressure
   on the button triggers the following successive functions:

   1. It swings the mirror out of the optical path, and closes the lens aperture
      to the preselected value,

   2. it operates the shutter,

   3. it reopens the aperture and returns the mirror to its original position.

   Do not attempt to wind the shutter before you have released the shutter
   release button.

3. The *shutter speed dial,* as its name implies, controls the shutter speed. It
   clicks into position opposite the engraved figures. The figure 1 represents
   1 second, all the other figures are the denominators of fractions of a second.
   Intermediate values can also be set continuously (exceptions: between 1/4

20

and $1/8$ sec and $1/30$ and $1/60$ sec). At the 'B' setting the shutter remains open as long as the release button is depressed. The symbol $\frac{\cancel{}}{}$ = $1/100$ sec indicates the highest shutter speed at which electronic flash synchronization is possible (see p. 26).

Controls for the left hand

The design of almost all lenses is identical. The aperture presetting ring is located directly next to the bayonet ring, i. e. close to the camera body. It can be rotated; the engraved white dot indicates the set aperture. In the 50mm Summicron-R the aperture scale ranges from f/2 to f/16, in other lenses from f/2.8 to f/22. The click-stops accommodate intermediate values halfways between the engraved figures. Intermediate values other than these should not be set. The next ring is fixed and has the depth-of-field scale engraved on it. The aperture numbers are entered on either side of the index mark ▲ for the focusing distances. Space is too restricted to permit the engraving of all the figures. The depth-of-field scale functions in connection with the distance scale. The distance values facing the aperture values to the left and right of the index show the depth-of-field range. At a large aperture (e. g. f/2) the range reproduced sharp in the photograph is small, at a small aperture (e. g. f/16) it is correspondingly larger. The extent of the depth of field is quicker and more convenient to read off the scale than off a table.

The setting ring for the focusing distance has two scales. The white scale is graduated in m, the red scale in ft. The reading is taken opposite the index (▲).

Distance setting ring ▷

Depth-of-field indicator ▷

Aperture presetting ring ▷

Left: Depth of field at f/4. Right: Depth of field at f/16.

Change in the depth of field when the aperture changes

The difference is particularly striking in photographs of architects' models etc. (p. 11). At a distance of 5m (16 ft 8in) at f/4 the depth of field ranges from 4m (13 ft 4in) to about 7m (about 23 ft). The next picture at f/16 presents a depth of field from 2.4m (8ft) to ∞. In the first case a shutter speed of $^1/_{500}$ sec can be used, whereas the corresponding value at f/16 is $^1/_{30}$ sec.

Although a large depth of field may be very convenient, it is often impossible to obtain. At slower shutter speeds the danger of camera shake increases. In practice, the lens should be stopped down just far enough for both requirements — sufficient depth of field and high enough shutter speed — to be reconciled. The most widely used apertures are f/4 - 5.6. - 8.

Automatic diaphragms

The automatic diaphragm of a Leicaflex lens opens and closes with the movements of the hinged mirror. The aperture presetting ring is rotated in order to preselect the lens aperture intended for the chosen shutter speed. Half values, too, can be set by click-stop. When the shutter button is pressed the aperture is closed to the preselected value, and automatically opened after the exposure. The image in the viewfinder is therefore always observed at full aperture.

22

Left: Unlocking the lens. Right: Inserting the lens.

Change of Lens

Leicaflex lenses can be changed at will, whether or not the camera shutter is wound, and irrespective of the distance and aperture setting. The right hand grips the fixed ring of the lens, rotating the lens to the left after the left thumb has released the lock on the camera body by pushing it back.

For the insertion of a lens, the red dot on the lens mount must face the red knob on the camera body. When both flanges are in proper contact give the lens a short twist to the right until you hear the bayonet click into position. Lenses should never be changed in direct sunlight; but in the shadow of your own body this operation is quite safe.

In all single-lens reflex cameras the mounts of the short- and standard-focal-length lenses are designed so that the surface of the rearmost member is exposed; it is therefore in danger of being soiled with finger marks. Always make sure that the glass surfaces are clean whenever you change lenses.

Lens hoods

can be of various shapes. They are part of the basic equipment of camera lenses. Some of them can be detached and replaced on the lens mount back-to-front. Make sure that the lens hood engages firmly; never hold the Leicaflex

◁ Lens hood

◁ Retaining ring

◁ Series filter (Size VI 41.5mm diam.
            Size VII 50.7mm diam.
            Size VIII 63.5mm diam.)

Lens thread in the 35mm Elmarit-R and
the 50mm Summicron-R.

Threads for mounting Series VI M 44 x 0.75
                            VII M 54 x 0.75
                            VIII M 72 x 0.75

by the lens hood. The long-focal-length Leicaflex lenses have permanently mounted extensible lens hoods, of which the later versions also function as filter holders.

Before inserting the filter slightly withdraw the knurled knob on the side of the lens hood; this allows the filter to be dropped into a plane position; it is secured as soon as the knurled knob is released.*

Series filters

Series filters differ from the conventional screw-in filters of the past in their smooth mount. They are merely inserted, and held in place by a special retaining ring or, with the later lenses, by the lens hood. The diameters of the series filters are standardized, the size is expressed in Roman numerals.

The table on p. 70 indicates the suitable filter sizes for all lenses. Where filters are secured by a retaining ring, this is first unscrewed and the filter inserted; the ring must now be screwed back in position. Unscrewing the ring is usually easy if the ring is held on one side only; this avoids internal strain.

---

* Attachment and removal of the new lens hood, p. 78.

24

Setting the film speed and the film indicator

Correct exposure measurement is possible only if the film speed is taken into account by the measuring mechanism. In Germany speed of a film is measured in DIN, internationally the ASA system is used. A film is twice as fast at a DIN rating increased by 3, half as fast when the rating is decreased by 3. The ASA system, on the other hand, is proportional, i. e. double the numerical value indicates double the speed. The setting ring (24) has DIN values and, on the opposite side, ASA values engraved upon it.

For adjustment the locking button (11) is depressed and the ring rotated until the number corresponding to the film speed faces the index mark. The setting range of the DIN values is 10–39, ASA values 8–6500. The symbols of the film indicator (9) have the following meaning: Black-and-white symbol = black-and-white film, sun = daylight colour film, bulb = artificial-light colour film, NEG = colour negative film. The locking button 11 serves as index mark.

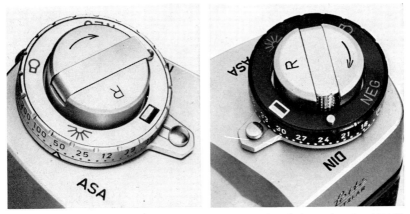

The DIN and ASA values are engraved on opposite sides of the setting ring (180°). The engraved dots without figures indicate intermediate values. The setting ring of the Leicaflex SL is black with white figures.

Flash synchronization

The very rapid action of the Leicaflex shutter permits electronic flash exposures up to $^1/_{100}$ sec (marked on the shutter speed dial with the flash symbol). For a focal-plane shutter this is extremely short. Naturally slower shutter speeds, too, can be used. Make sure to connect the cable with the socket marked with the flash symbol on the front of the camera body (see p. 28,8); the socket below, marked with a bulb symbol, is provided for the majority of flashbulbs.

The two sockets differ in that the electronic flash is triggered when the first roller blind of the shutter has almost completed its movement; in the flashbulb socket the flash is triggered while the first roller blind is still moving. This allows for the firing delay of the flashbulbs, which differs with the dimension and type of the lamp, the average being in the region of $^1/_{60}$ sec.

The table below lists various flashbulbs with their recommended shutter speeds. Since the trigger action of each flash socket functions independently of the other, electronic flash and a flashbulb can be used simultaneously with the Leicaflex. The standardized coaxial plugs as supplied with the conventional flash units fit the Leicaflex sockets. In some flashbulb units the capacitor is charged only if a lateral or central contact is made by the accessory shoe. This should be borne in mind during the purchase of a flashbulb unit.

	Electronic flash	B→ ⚡ (=$^1/_{100}$)	⚡
	M 2	1→$^1/_{30}$	Contact bush (top)
Flashbulbs	Flash Cubes **A G 1 B** **A G 3 B**	1→$^1/_{60}$	Contact bush (bottom)
	XM1 B **PF 1 B** **PF 5 B**	1→$^1/_{125}$	
	GE 5 **25** **M 3** **PF 60 B**	1→$^1/_{250}$	

The first version of the Leicaflex (discontinued)

Manipulation does not differ a great deal from that of the Leicaflex SL. But to avoid confusion the two versions are treated separately on the following pages. The different features are the exposure measurement, the viewfinder screen, and film insertion. The lenses for the Leicaflex SL have a second cam for the exposure measurement, but can be used equally well in the Leicaflex.

The designation and location of the various controls will be found on the following pages.

The sectional drawing below shows the optical path inside the Leicaflex. The mirror and the observation system with Fresnel disc, field lens, prism and eyelens serve only for viewing the image. The mirror is swung out of the optical path immediately before the exposure.

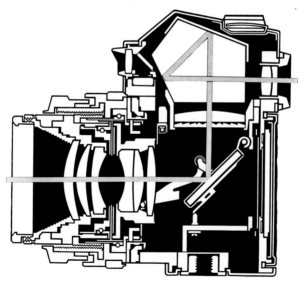

In this cross-sectional drawing the dotted line indicates the optical path for observation. The pentaprism erects the image, producing a right-way-round view.

1 Eyelets for the neck strap
2 Self-timer (delayed-action mechanism)
3 Preselection lever for the mirror movement
4 Lens bayonet lock
5 Cover for the Mallory battery of the exposure meter
6 Exposure meter window
7 Button for testing the Mallory battery
8 Flash contacts
9 Film indicator
10 Folding rewind crank
11 Locking button for the DIN/ASA setting
12 Accessory shoe
13 Transport lever, also switching the exposure meter on and off

14 Shutter release button with cable release bush
15 Automatic frame counter
16 Shutter speed dial
17 Depth-of-field scale
18 Aperture presetting ring
19 Distance setting ring
20 Red knob for lens change
21 Rewind release button
22 ¹/₄in tripod bush
23 Locking bar for the hinged camera back
24 DIN/ASA scale
25 Viewfinder eyelens. A correction lens mount for users with defective eyesight can be attached.

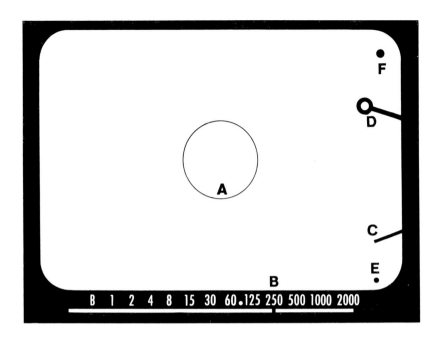

A look through the viewfinder

In the large, clear Leicaflex viewfinder you can see all the adjustments for picture area, sharpness, and shutter speed (marked by letters). These controls are simple and quick to handle.

A = focusing circle with micro-prisms,

B = mark of the set shutter speed,

C = measuring pointer,

D = follow pointer,

E = small dot for battery test,

F = large dot.

During the adjustment of the aperture presetting ring the follow pointer moves towards the large dot when the aperture is opend, and towards the small ring when it is closed. The follow pointer is also coupled with the shutter speeds.

How to focus

The focusing area is surrounded by a black circle; it consists of more than 13 000 microprisms, which diffuse the incident light rays that are not exactly in focus, so that you can clearly distinguish sharpness and unsharpness.

Focus the object by rotating the focusing ring on the lens. The light in the microprisms will flicker as long as the image is unsharp; flickering stops only when the object is correctly focused.

Normally, the helical mount of the lens is rotated for focusing. But with short distances (below 40in (1m) for 35mm and 50mm; below 80in (2m) for 90mm and 135mm focal length) the following method is preferable. Set the helical mount of the lens at the desired distance and sway backwards and forwards with the camera until the object appears sharp in the focusing field. Readiness for action is definitely improved by this method. The procedure should, however, be practised repeatedly.

With a 35mm lens distances above 80in (2m) can be estimated with sufficient confidence provided the lighting conditions are good. When using wide-angle lenses you will find it a great advantage to familiarize yourself with their depth-of-field range; this vastly increases your action-readiness.

Critical focusing is one of the most important points in handling a camera. You can use three different methods of focusing a single-lens reflex camera:

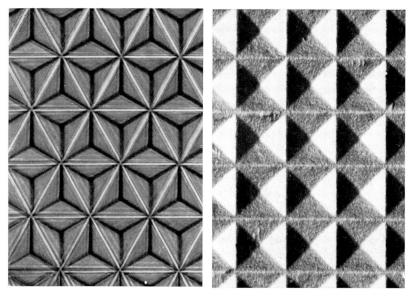

The diameter of the focusing circle is 7mm. In the first version of the Leicaflex the screen pattern consists of triangular micro-pyramids, whereas the SL model has square ones. The illustration shows sections of the two screens at a magnification of about 200x.

1. on the groundglass screen, 2. with the aid of a measuring wedge, and 3. through microprisms. In the Leicaflex the last of the three methods has been adopted, because its focusing accuracy is about the same as that of the measuring wedge. But it does not have the latter's disadvantage of introducing a disturbing feature, which remains disturbing even after focusing, in the centre of the viewfinder image. With the prism screen, on the other hand, flickering stops once the image is in focus, so that only the fine circle marking the measuring field proper remains visible.

When the aperture is too small, measuring wedges and micro-prisms become black, because their plane angles are matched to definite lens apertures. $f/5.6$ has been found to be a useful setting. Neither of the two methods can be employed with smaller apertures. In the Leicaflex the lenses are therefore used at full aperture for observation and focusing. See also pp. 48.

Venus de Milo, Louvre, Paris. 50mm Summicron-R, f/2.8, 1/30sec, ordinary daylight.

Battery testing and -change

The built-in exposure meter functions on the principle of the photo-resistor. This has the advantages of higher limiting sensitivity, i.e. accuracy of measurement even in bad lighting conditions, and a narrower angle and therefore more favourable picture area for measuring.

But unlike the conventional selenium cells of earlier exposure meters a photo-resistor depends on a current source. For the Leicaflex the Mallory PX 625 battery with the white ring has been chosen for this purpose. Current consumption is negligible and changes with the intensity of the light incident on the photo-resistor. Maximum light intensity produces maximum current flux. Normally the battery has a life of 1–2 years. To replace it unscrew the cap (5) on the front, and remove it; the new battery is in the correct position if the engraving is visible after insertion.

If you find it impossible to obtain a 'Mallory PX 625', you can use a 'Mallory PX 13' at temperatures above freezing point. A difference between the two batteries is noticeable at temperatures below freezing point only. The 'PX 625'

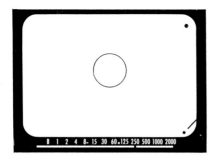

This is the position of the measuring pointer when the button next to the field window of the viewfinder on the front of the camera is pressed for testing the Mallory battery. If the voltage is too low the pointer will not be deflected as far as the black dot. A difference of up to 1 pointer width is admissible. Deflection of the pointer beyond the black dot can be ignored.

is more cold-resistant and can be used at a minimum temperature of − 10° C (14° F). But the exposure meter will continue to function even in colder temperatures provided you prevent the battery from cooling below −10° C (14° F).

Exposure measurement

The measuring pointer of the exposure meter moves along the right-hand edge of the viewfinder window. Measurements should be taken in the horizontal camera position even for vertical pictures. For correct exposure measurement the follow pointer must be brought into register with the measuring pointer. The follow pointer is coupled with both the diaphragm presetting ring of the lens and the shutter speed dial. You can therefore either preset the shutter speed and adapt the lens aperture, or determine the lens aperture and adjust the follow pointer with the shutter speed dial.

The shutter speed setting is visible along the lower edge of the viewfinder window, providing an important clue whether it is fast enough for the sharp rendering of a moving subject, or too slow to prevent the danger of camera shake. If you want to check the depth of field before making the exposure, all you have to do is to read its values off the depth-of-field scale of the lens. An aperture indication in the viewfinder would by itself not be sufficient to obtain this information.

The measuring angle of the exposure meter is identical with the angle of field of a 90mm lens. With lenses of shorter focal lengths therefore only part of the picture area is measured. Far from being a drawback, this is actually an advantage.

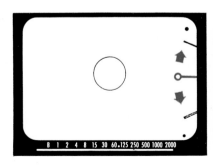 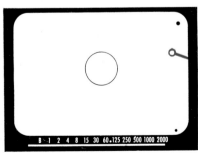

Wide-angle and standard lenses often cover, e. g. with landscape subjects, large expanses of sky, which are not characteristic during the determination of the exposure time. Built-in exposure meters measure the sum of the reflected light within a certain acceptance angle. They are calibrated on a standard object that reflects $1/6$ (about 17 %; of the incident brightness. This corresponds to a dark grey surface. The determination of the exposure time is the more accurate the closer the similarity between camera subject and standard object. Since deviations of up to half an aperture stop are generally accommodated by the exposure latitude of the photographic material, corrections are necessary only if the camera subject differs greatly from the standard.

It is true that in black-and-white photography the method of development influences the final result. In order to compensate, for instance, very contrasty contre-jour subjects it is recommended to expose generously and cut down development. In 35mm photography, however, these differences in contrast are normally disregarded, because on a film of 36 exposures the subjects differ so widely that this rule is impracticable. Here we apply the principle of choosing our exposure time so that it is not at the lower limit, but has a reserve of one aperture stop. This reserve should not be used except in an emergency, and even then only if practically the whole film contains the same type ob subject, for instance when you take photographs during a jolly party in the evening or during a small family occasion in ordinary room lighting; with slightly extended treatment in fresh developer solution a 400 ASA (27 DIN) film can then be exposed as for 800 ASA (30 DIN) with complete success. But this method should not be used indiscriminately; contre-jour subjects, for instance, would produce excessively contrasty negatives.

The exposure meter is misled when the contrast range (ratio of the brightest and darkest portions of the subject) is too large, for instance, when you look out of a room at a sunlit landscape. It is impossible to render both room and landscape correctly because the brightness range exceeds the tone range of the bromide paper. If the landscape is to be reproduced correctly you must take your exposure meter reading near the window; if the interior is the pictorially important feature, you must eliminate the effect of the bright landscape almost entirely.

There are other cases in which your exposure measurement may be faulty, because the brightness of your camera subject differs radically from that of

The field inside the frame indicates the measuring angle of the exposure meter when a 50mm lens is used. The field corresponds to a focal length of 90mm.

the standard object. Snowscapes are frequent examples. On the assumption that a snow-covered landscape consists of more than 70% snow area the reflections of the incident light will be not 17% as in the standard object, but 60—80%. The pointer of the exposure meter will indicate 2 aperture stops smaller than at normal intensity of illumination. Now the argument that you may give a shorter exposure for bright snow than for a standard object is correct; the difficulty is that you should in fact increase your exposure over that indicated by the exposure meter by one stop. Snow pictures of no more than 50% proportion of snow are, however, correctly exposed at the measured exposure time.

On a sandy beach, too, reflection may be higher because of the high reflecting power of the tiny quartz crystals of the sand. But conditions are only very rarely as unfavourable as in snow, for instance if the subject consists almost entirely of white sand. Normally, if the blue sky occupies half the picture area, correction of the exposure value is no longer necessary.

The situation is exactly reversed in night subjects, indoor figure skating displays etc., where only small portions of the picture area intensely illuminated and the surroundings are hidden in darkness. The Leicaflex exposure meter has a measuring angle identical with the angle of field of a 90mm lens. If the light/dark ratio within the measuring angle deviates from the standard you will be able to make a correction by reducing the exposure. Here, too, it will mostly be only one aperture stop. If the object can be approached more closely, so that normal conditions exist within the angle of measurement, the measurement will be correct.

These corrections, incidentally, are necessary with all exposure meters employing the method of integrated measurement irrespective whether this is taken through the camera lens or, as in the earlier Leicaflex, outside the lens.

The limiting sensitivity of the Leicaflex exposure meter is 6.3 asb (asb = apostilb, measuring unit of luminous density of reflected light). Translated into exposure values, an exposure time corresponding to 1 sec at f/2.8 for a 40 ASA (17 DIN) film can still be measured. This limiting sensitivity can be slightly increased if a reading of a sheet of white paper is taken instead of that of the object itself. The author uses this method in poorly lit interiors, because it calls for a close approach to the object. The exposure meter is moved to within about 6in (15cm) of the paper so that no shadow is cast on the white area to be measured. The exposure time thus found will have to be corrected since the reflection of the paper is about 4 x stronger than that of the standard object; the diaphragm must therefore be opened 2 stops or a 4 x slower shutter speed chosen, e.g. 1 sec instead of ¹/₄ sec at a given aperture.

The slowest instantaneous speed that can be set on the shutter speed dial is 1 sec; if still slower speeds are required, for instance for interiors at small apertures, a simple conversion is necessary. If possible, the measurement should be taken at full aperture. The shutter speed must be halved (= the exposure time doubled) for each step the aperture is stopped down. An example will illustrate the adjustment. The measurement was 1 sec at f/2.8. In the sequence below you will find the corresponding apertures and shutter speeds above and below the line respectively:

Two examples of unusual conditions of exposure measurement.
Left: Figure skating display. The narrow spotlight beams illuminate only the skaters from several directions. The surroundings are in almost complete darkness. The proportion of the illuminated area in the whole picture is very small. Ordinary measurement indicates far too long an exposure because it allows for the dark portions of the subject.
Right: Downhill skier in contre-jour. Here the situation is reversed. The proportion of white is too large, the exposure meter gives too short an exposure, because its response to the abundance of white is higher than is necessary for a correct exposure. If the proportion of snow is 70% and more, use the next larger aperture than indicated (e. g. f/8 instead of f/11).

Aperture	2,8	4	5,6	8	11	16	22
Shutter speed (sec)	1	2	4	8	16	32	64

The arrangement and measurement method of the Leicaflex exposure meter has been found extremely reliable in practice. Its main advantage consists in the speed at which the correct result is reached. It has its limitations in the extreme close-up range when the parallax between camera lens and exposure meter becomes effective, and with very long-focal-length lenses.

Selector lever for the mirror movement

Position I (lever pointing upwards) = normal mirror position. The mirror is swung up immediately before the exposure, and instantly swung back into the optical path afterwards.

Position II (lever pointing outwards) = the mirror is arrested in the upward position to permit subsequent serial exposures.

Position III (lever pointing downwards) = the mirror is swung out of the optical path before the shutter is released:

a) if the shutter is wound, by means of switching to Position III,

b) if the shutter is not wound, by means of winding the shutter.
After the last serial exposure the mirror must be swung back into the optical path by a change of the lever to Position I *before* the shutter is wound.

The self-timer

The *self-timer*, also called delayed-action mechanism, produces a delay of 8—10 seconds. It is wound by rotation of lever (2) through 180°, and released by pressure on the shutter release button of the camera. All shutter speeds can be set before the self-timer is wound. Make certain that the Leicaflex shutter is wound.

In brilliant contre jour, sunlight and powder snow have this fascinating, plastic effect.
Photograph by Prof. F. Hoppichler

Film insertion

Naturally, inserting the film is quite simple, and much quicker than can be explained here. However, do practise it at a fixed sequence with a control, so that you can rely on correct film transport.

Open the camera back

Depress the safety button, simultaneously pushing the locking bar upwards. The camera back opens and can be swung through 180°; at the same time, the frame counter sets itself at the second line to the left of zero. Push the shaft of the rewind crank upwards — pull enough film out of the cartridge for 5–6 perforation holes along the lower edge of the film to be exposed — grip film end, emulsion side upwards, between right thumb and forefinger. Hold the take-up spool with the left thumb so that one of the slots faces upwards, push the trimmed film end into the slot so that the perforated edge lies flush against the flange of the take-up spool.

Insert the film cartridge and secure it by pushing the rewind crank in. Wind the film by means of the winding lever (if necessary release the shutter first), and ensure that the sprockets of the transport drum engage in the perforation holes. Keep the winding lever taut until the camera back is closed.

Closing the camera back and testing film insertion

Push the locking bar downwards until it engages. Wind the film through two frames.The film has been correctly inserted if the rewind crank moves against the direction of the arrow as the film is wound on. Take up the slack of the 20-exposure film in the cartridge by rotating the rewind crank in the direction of the arrow. After the third film wind the camera is ready for action.

Film removal

Once the last frame has been exposed the rapid winding lever can no longer be moved. The film must be rewound: First press the rewind release button on the camera baseplate, so that the transport drum can turn freely Swing out — do not pull out — the rewind crank and rotate it in the direction of the arrow only, until the film is rewound after a slight resistance has been overcome. As a control, the frame counter also runs backwards. Open the camera body, pull up the rewind crank, and remove the cartridge.

Open camera back. The locking bar can be pushed up only when the round safety button is depressed.

Insert the film cartridge. It is best to begin with pushing the film end into the slot of the take-up spool before placing the film cartridge into the space provided for it.

Pushing in the rewind crank holds the cartridge in position. While the camera is still open, wind a short length of film to make sure that the teeth of the transport sprocket drum at the bottom engage the perforations of the film.

Rewind film. You can turn the rewind crank in the direction of the arrow only after pressing the button on the underside of the camera. — The film in the cartridge is better protected against light if the film end has not been wound back into it completely. To prevent mistaking it for an un-exposed film, you can mark the end of the exposed film by folding it sharply.

THE LEICAFLEX SL

Why selective light metering?

The two Leicaflex models differ mainly in the method of their exposure measurement. Of the widely varying ways of measuring the brightness of a photographic subject, none produces 100% correct results automatically. This is less the fault of the exposure meters than due to the fact that our photographic subjects range from a sunlit glacier in contre-jour light to a night picture in moonlight, and that besides the brightness the contrast of the subject plays a particularly important part. By contrast we mean the brightness difference between the brightest and darkest portion of the subject.

With a built-in exposure meter the reflected light is measured, either within a fixed angle or, if the measurement is obtained through the lens, within the angle of field of this particular lens. At first sight, through-the-lens measurement appears to be the only reliable one. But if you examine the results and above all the various methods you will find that here, too, considerable deviations occur.

If you take an integrating reading, i. e. a reading of the sum total of the light incident on the entire picture area, the subject contrast has a considerable, and possibly disturbing, effect. To eliminate such disturbances a small area has been chosen for the measurement in the Leicaflex SL. The inner circle of the viewfinder, of 7mm diameter, includes the measuring field. This is lined up with an area suitable for the exposure measurement, and the follow pointer registered with the measuring pointer; this is all you need do to find the correct exposure time. It is a quick, accurate, and reliable method, but it requires you to become familiar with the brightness values of the subject to be photographed. You will learn very quickly what areas are suitable for measurement. A special chapter on p. 54 with many examples of pictures is devoted to the explanation of this important process.

The Leicaflex SL has a novel focusing screen. In addition to the central prism-screen measuring field it has a matt microscreen in the surrounding area, which can also be used for focusing. The location of the depth of field is now also possible; simply press the new depth-of-field button; this closes the diaphragm to the preset aperture value.

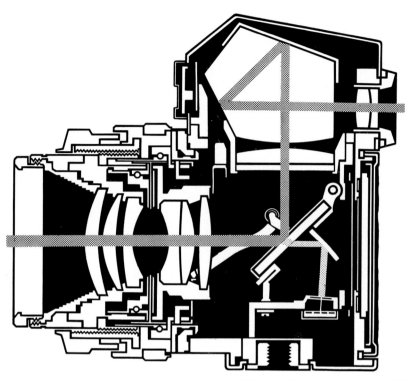

This sectional diagram shows the most important differences between the Leicaflex SL and the earlier Leicaflex. The oberservation mirror does not reflect all the light, transmitting about 20 %, which reaches a second mirror; this directs it to the photocell in the bottom of the camera.

This principle has the important advantage that the exposure measurement is not affected by disturbing stray light above the viewfinder window. The photocell is located so far to one side of the semitransparent mirror that no stray light enters it.

The main proportion of the light is directed into the viewfinder system as before. The earlier Fresnel rings near the focusing plane have been replaced by a spherical surface on the focusing prism to produce the necessary refraction.

1 Eyelets for the neck strap
2 Self-timer (delayed-action mechanism)
4 Bayonet lock for the lens
5 Cover for the Mallory battery for the exposure meter
7 Button for testing the Mallory battery
8 Flash contacts
9 Film indicator
10 Folding rewind crank
11 Locking button for the DIN/ASA setting
12 Accessory shoe
13 Transport lever, also switching the exposure meter on and off

14 Shutter release button, with cable release bush
15 Automatic frame counter
16 Shutter speed dial
17 Depth-of-field scale
18 Aperture presetting ring
19 Distance setting ring
20 Red knob for lens change
21 Rewind release button
22 ¹/₄ in tripod bush
23 Locking bar for the hinged camera back
24 DIN/ASA scale
25 Viewfinder eyelens. A correction lens mount for users with defective eyesight can be attached
26 Depth-of-field button

The viewfinder and focusing in the Leicaflex SL

The important exposure controls are adjusted in the large Leicaflex viewfinder, where picture area and sharpness are checked and corrected. The measuring field, within a circle of 7mm diameter, occupies the centre of the viewfinder field. It contains thousands of microprisms, which diffuse the light rays so long as the sighted object is not exactly focused. The correct distance is found by rotation of the focusing ring on the lens. The image becomes steady and contrasty, and ceases to flicker as soon as it is sharply focused. In the Leicaflex SL the field surrounding the viewfinder circle has a very fine matt texture and is therefore also suitable for focusing. In this feature it considerably differs from the viewfinder of the earlier Leicaflex. The other functions are shown in the illustration on p. 30 and explained on pp. 30 to 32.

Focusing accuracy in all reflex cameras depends largely on the visual acuity of the user. Many of us have slightly defective eyesight, but not disturbing enough to require the wearing of spectacles. It should be borne in mind that the recently introduced eye test for applicants for a German driving licence has revealed that about one third of the persons tested do not enjoy full visual acuity.

Should you experience difficulties with your focusing, these may be due to slightly faulty vision. Correction lenses to compensate for such faults are available. They are specially mounted for slipping onto the viewfinder eyepiece. When ordering correction lenses, please state the dioptres of your distance spectacles. Spectacle wearers using their distance spectacles do not require correction lenses.

Photography with ultra-long-focal-length lenses is most fascinating.

The transition unsharpness-sharpness-unsharpness must be calculated into the pictorial composition. To be able to use this effect with confidence in pictorial composition, you should throughly familiarize yourself with it through many trial exposures. Incidentally, the minimum distances at which animals feel safe and unmolested vary widely.

This Sacred Ibis was observed and photographed by J. Behnke from a distance of about 130ft (40m); 560mm Telyt f/5.6; f/5.6, ¹/₅₀₀sec; Televit rapid focusing device.

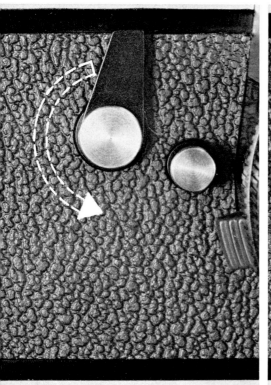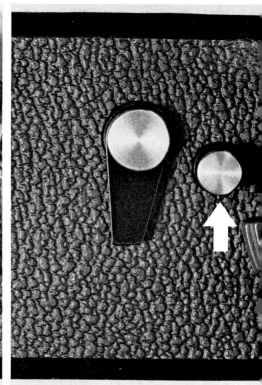

The self-timer (delayed-action mechanism) and the depth-of-field button

The self-timer, also called delayed-action mechanism, introduces a delay of 8—10 seconds between the pressing of the button and shutter action. The action is delayed by anti-clockwise rotation of the lever through 180° (see illustration). Depress the shutter release button for actuation of the self-timer. It is impossible to release the shutter directly when the self-timer is wound up.

Unless the winding lever has been rotated through 180°, the release button may be blocked even if the lever has been returned to its rest position by hand. Remedy: fully wind self-timer and actuate it with the release button. Pressure on the depth-of-field button closes the lens diaphragm to the setting effective during the exposure. It is now possible to check in the viewfinder the

50

depth of field to be expected in the picture. The lenses for the Leicaflex SL have a special cam, which transmits the aperture value to the exposure meter. In these lenses the depth-of-field button must not be pressed during exposure measurement if they are designed for measurement at full aperture. Only when the measurement is to be carried out at the working aperture must the button be pressed while the exposure is being measured.

Battery testing and change

The exposure meter of the Leicaflex SL, too, uses a photo-resistor as a photo-cell. The most important points as described on p. 34 are also applicable here. The battery is now located in the baseplate of the camera. Mallory PX 625 and PX 13 batteries are suitable for the Leicaflex SL.

To test the state of the battery, look through the viewfinder (horizontal position) and depress the little button (7) at the side of the prism attachment. With undervoltage, the pointer of the exposure meter will not be fully deflected to the black dot in the bottom right-hand corner of the viewfinder field. A difference of the width of the pointer can be ignored, deflection beyond the black dot is without significance.

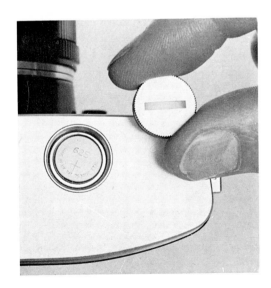

The Mallory battery is housed below this cover, which can be easily unscrewed by means of a coin. Insert the battery with the lettering facing you.

Film insertion and unloading

Film insertion has become even easier and more convenient in the Leicaflex SL. Since reliable film transport depends on correct film insertion you should pay particular attention to this procedure.

Wind the shutter and press the button. Open the camera back.

Depress safety button, at the same time push the locking bar upwards. The camera back snaps open, and can be turned through 180°. Push the spindle of the rewind crank upwards — pull enough film out of the cassette for 5–6 perforations on the lower film edge to appear — grip film end (emulsion side upwards) between right thumb and index finger, and push the trimmed film end into one of the slots of the take-up spool from above so that the perforated edge is perfectly flush with the flange of the take-up spool.

Turn the film cartridge round and insert it in the space provided for it. Push the rewind crank in; the cartridge is now held in position. Wind the film by means of the winding lever and make sure that the sprocket teeth engage the perforation holes. Keep the winding lever taut until you have closed the camera back, which in the Leicaflex SL is self-locking.

Wind the film through one frame, turn the rewind crank against the direction of the arrow until you feel a slight resistance. This is essential especially with a 20-exposure cartridge. Release the shutter. During the next winding action the rewind crank must rotate backwards. This is an important control for correct function. The camera is ready for action after three windings; the frame counter is now set at 1.

Unloading the film

After the last frame has been exposed, the rapid winding lever can no longer be operated. The film must be rewound; first press the rewind release button in the baseplate of the camera, so that the transport sprocket drum can rotate freely. Swing out (do not pull out) the rewind crank, and turn it in the direction of the arrow until the film, after a slight resistance is felt, is rewound. The frame counter turns backwards as a control. Open the camera body, pull up the rewind crank, and take out the cartridge.

1 Open camera back. The locking bar can be pushed up only after the round safety button is depressed.

2 Insert the film cartridge. Push the film end (emulsion side up) into one of the slots of the take-up spool from above.

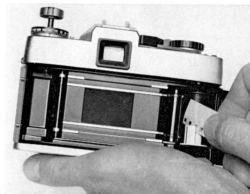

3 Place the film cartridge into the space provided for it. Pushing in the rewind crank holds the cartridge in position. While the camera is still open, wind a short length of film to make sure that the teeth of the transport sprocket drum at the bottom engage the perforations of the film.

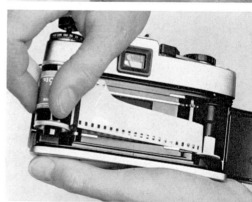

4 Rewind film. You can turn the rewind crank in the direction of the arrow only after pressing the button on the underside of the camera.

Selective exposure measurement

In the Leicaflex SL the exposure is measured through the lens. The observation mirror is semitransparent, and in the central field a concave-cylindrical mirror measuring about 12 x 18 mm is hinged to it. It directs the light to the photo-resistor situated in the bottom of the cast housing. This position has a number of advantages. The film plane would be ideal for the measurement; however, the photo-resistor is situated a little further away than this. Light that does not enter through the lens, but through the observation prism, could disturb and falsify the measurement. In the Leicaflex SL, however, the photo-resistor is located so far to the rear that it cannot be reached by any stray light. If all the light that contributes to the formation of the image is measured proportionately, we speak of integrating measurement. By and large this is a satisfactory method; faulty measurements can occur only when the subject is very contrasty. Here, the method of aimed, selective measurement is vastly superior. Exposure determination is 100% reliable when a reading is taken of a pictorially important element.

The exposure meter is switched on and off with the film transport lever. It is switched off when the lever is in the parked position against the camera body. To switch it on, move the lever slightly to the right. Measurement is more accurate if you hold the camera horizontally, because slight differences in weight will make themselves felt in the measuring instrument if the camera is rotated through 90°. The deviations are, however, small.

The measuring field of the exposure meter corresponds to the central field of the focusing screen; it has a diameter of 7mm i. e. about $^1/_6$ of the picture diagonal. The measuring angle of the exposure meter therefore changes with the angle of view every time the lens is changed. With the 135mm Elmarit-R f/2.8, for instance, the angle of view is 18°, and the measuring angle of the exposure meter 3°.

The measuring pointer of the exposure meter moves along the right-hand edge of the viewfinder image. For the correct exposure measurement the follow pointer must be made to coincide with the exposure meter pointer. It is coupled with both the diaphragm presetting ring and the shutter speed dial. You may therefore preselect either the shutter speed or the lens aperture according to preference. The shutter speed is indicated on a scale along the bottom edge of the viewfinder field. You will find the relevant illustrations on pp. 34/35.

Our eye is capable of very rapid adaptation to various brightness values; but it can evaluate only comparative, not absolute, differences in brightness. In sunlight outdoors, for instance, you can easily remember some standard exposures. But immediately you enter interiors the situation becomes difficult. The wish for a reliable exposure meter has therefore been of long standing. With separate exposure meters we distinguish between two methods of measurement: either the incident light is measured, or the light reflected by the subject. With all exposure meters built into the camera it is usual to measure the reflected light. For the calibration of an exposure meter a reflection of 17 % of the total incident light is assumed as standard.

Many subjects occur in practical photography which differ in their reflection values. This is not significant provided the deviation does not exceed certain limits. Even colour reversal films with their narrow exposure latitude can accommodate half a stop. The conventional integrating measurement, in which the sum of the reflected light is measured, is extremely common. It is very convenient and yields an acceptable exposure time in 80 % of all cases without the need for special consideration. The only difficulties occur when the subject is unusual. The importance of the aimed selective measurement, possible in the Leicaflex SL, increases with the contrast of the photographic subject. Selected-area measurement constitutes the best method especially with interesting subjects of large brightness differences, e. g. in contre-jour light, night shots, in the circus, or with pantomimes on ice, interiors by the window, etc. The simple condition you have to meet is this: point the circular measuring field of the Leicaflex SL at an area which is suitable for the measurement of the exposure time. A number of examples will illustrate the applications of this principle in practice. The central field of the Leicaflex SL viewfinder constitutes the measuring field both for focusing the subject and for determining the exposure time. It is of course possible to choose two different subject areas for these procedures.

As already mentioned the correct exposure time largely depends not only on the quantity of the reflected light, but also on the contrast. The power of reflection and the surface structure and therefore the appearance of the subject change according to the distance of the light sources and the angle of the incident light.

The following example, a right-angle, isosceles triangle, shows the same grey steps on the right and on the left. The three illustrations make it clear how the subject contrast changes owing to the differential intensity of the illumination.

Top: 2 identical light sources at a distance of 20in (50cm) illuminate the two lateral surfaces of the triangle from the left and from the right. The walnut casts a weak shadow on either side, but there is no 'roundness', no feeling of space. Measurement of the grey steps on the left and right produces identical values. The ratio of illumination is 1:1.

Middle: Set-up and camera viewpoint are unchanged. But the distance of the light source illuminating the right side has been increased to 40in (1m). This side therefore receives only $1/4$ of the original light. This produces clear shadows and a plastic rendering. By means of selective area measurement you can measure the lighting contrast already at the exposure stage; it is 1:4.

Bottom: The lamp on the right has been removed to a distance of 80in (2m). Illumination on the right is insufficient. Here, too, you could measure the difference at the exposure stage and take countermeasures, for a difference of illumination of 1:16* is unsuitable for normal purposes.

These differences are visible more clearly on this sequence of pictures than to your eye looking at the original object. Results of the exposure measurement will noticeably differ with the measuring method. If you measure according to the principle of integration, the entire quantity of light on the subject is measured. Here the deviations are smaller as one would suspect from the differences in illumination between the upper and the lower picture. But with the selective measurement of the Leicaflex SL you can take readings both of the bright and the dark side as you wish, and choose the exposure time suitable for the task in hand. In our case the same exposure time was chosen for all

---

* Incidentally: on the walnut the lighting contrast is not 1:16, the white background being responsible for a considerable softening of the shadows.

three pictures, because the difference in the falling-off of brightness on the right had to be shown clearly. The reading was taken of the area on the left marked by a circle. Its graduation corresponds very well to the requirements for average brightness.

In ordinary black-and-white photography naturally many situations arise in which detail and reproduction of the grey scale in the bottom picture, right, is essential. You will be able to accomplish this on the negative without difficulty by appropriately increasing the exposure time. The situation is more difficult in positive reproduction on paper. If you compensate excessive contrast by printing the negative on a soft grade of paper, the grey steps on the left and right will become flat. The difference in reflection within a grey scale between "white" and "black" is approximately 1:30. Owing to the difference in the illumination the ratio of "white left" and "black right" is increased to 1:120 in the centre and to 1:480 in the bottom picture. Since in the positive, too, only about 1:30 can be rendered correctly, you should, when faced with large brightness differences, decide which portions are pictorially important and base your exposure on them. You can now do this with great accuracy by means of the selective measurement in the Leicaflex SL. The situation is somewhat different with colour reversal film. It is true that in projection a brightness range considerably longer than 1:30 can be reproduced satisfactorily, but the reversal process is so finely balanced that the light portions (called "highlights" by the expert) will be burnt out, they will be empty, devoid of detail if the exposure had been too generous. Giving a generous exposure is therefore pointless if highlight detail is lost for the sake of good shadow detail. Even if the lighting contrast is high exposure should be based on the left-hand grey scale as indicated by the index circle.

The next example, too, clearly demonstrates the reliability of selective light measurement. The same subject is shown four times, only the background has been changed. The exposure time remains the same in each case, because the varying brightness of the background does not affect the measurement. Here, too, the area measured is the one enclosed in the circle.

With integrating measurement of the entire picture area the difference in brightness would have a noticeable influence on the reading. Especially to the white background the exposure meter reacts vigorously and indicates a shorter exposure (higher shutter speed or smaller aperture), because a 'brilliant'

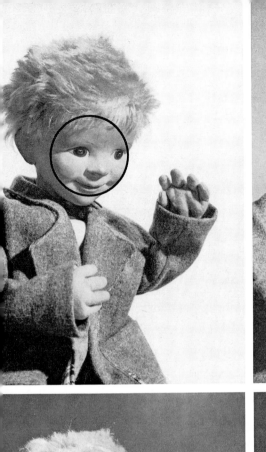

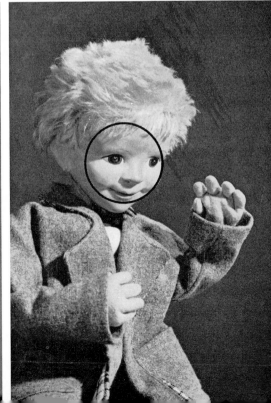

white will be obtained in such cases only if the white background receives extra illumination.

In the picture above, the index circle encloses an area which is suitable for the exposure measurement. It is, however, by no means the only suitable area, for the advice simply states: "Choose an area of medium brightness".

Naturally the viewfinder shows that the various portions of our subject have greatly differing reflecting powers; the white clouds are considerably brighter than the shadows of the wooden chalets. The pointer of the exposure meter reacts to every brightness difference. This need not disturb you; after all, these differences must be visible in your picture. What you must not do is measure the extremes. The white clouds, for instance, indicate an exposure too short by 2 aperture stops; measurement of the shadows of the chalets, on the other hand, indicates far too long an exposure.

To photograph an interior with a view through the window is one of the more difficult subjects for the camera, because the brightness range far exceeds the normal value. What your eye accommodates without any effort becomes a

problem for the camera. The brightness difference between indoors and out-doors often amounts to 7 or more light values. The following scale gives the intensity distribution of the light values:

Light values	1	2	3	4	5	6	7	8	9	10	11	12
Light intensity	2	4	8	16	32	64	128	256	512	1024	2048	4096

Each successive number indicates a doubling of the brightness.

If an interior requires a shutter speed of 1sec at f/8, f/8 and $^1/_{250}$sec might be correct for the landscape outside the window. You must therefore choose between indoors and out. If the interior is to have good detail in the picture, the exterior portions are mostly overexposed. If you try to use a medium value, the interior portion will still be underexposed. A balance can be established only by means of additional light (flash). Exposure measurement, too, has up to now been difficult, but the problem has been solved by the advent of the Leicaflex SL with its selective measurement. Simply choose a suitable portion not directly bordering on the window.

Besides the many average subjects of a long range of brightness steps from white to black, there are, of course, those of a very limited range. The most important examples are snowscapes, and winter sports subjects. Here portions of medium brightness are often missing. In full sunlight at high altitudes the reflection of the snow is so intense that the pointer of the exposure meter is deflected beyond the limiting value. Open shadow portions in the snow should be measured as indicated by the circle above. If the subject has no suitable field at all, as in the picture on the right, take your reading off the palm of a hand in sunlight. If persons form part of a winter subject, a red anorak will give a correct exposure value, whereas an equally bright blue anorak may indicate a somewhat generous exposure. The reason for this is the difference between the spectral sensitivity of the photo-resistors and that of our photographic emulsions. The photo-resistors are less sensitive to blue, and more sensitive to red than our photographic materials. This fact also makes itself felt when filters are used. Measurement behind an orange filter extends the exposure time by the factor 2, whereas the filter factor is 3. With the ordinary yellow filter, however, the deviation is so small as to be negligible.

On a photographic safari J. Behnke photographed this lion in a tree. This picture effectively demonstrates the advantages of using a selected area for your exposure measurement. A long-focal-length lens (180mm) is in the camera as the subject distance is large, and for this reason alone a close-up reading is out of the question here. The lion is in the shadow, and the sky in the background is so bright that an integrating exposure measurement would produce much too short an exposure time. The measurement of the area within the circle gives perfect results.

Metering at the working aperture

Metering at full aperture as provided with the 2-cam lenses offers so many advantages that we strongly advise you to have your earlier Leicaflex lenses fitted with the second cam if you wish to use them in the Leicaflex SL. The modification is carried out in our factory.

In the exceptional case of having to use a lens with only one cam, you can take your exposure reading at the working aperture; at the same time you have to press the depth-of-field button. Because the new measuring system starts from a limit stop, which is not incorporated in these lenses, a small deviation will occur. You can compensate this by rating the film speed slower by 2 DIN (deduct ⅓ from the ASA rating).

With some accessories, such as the new focusing bellows, the Televit-R, the adapter ring *14127, and the ring combination *14134, the working aperture must always be used for exposure measurement. Earlier versions of the two last-named accessories, too, must be modified in the factory for use with the Leicaflex SL; when they have an * before their code number this modification is not necessary, as they are already suitable for the Leicaflex SL.

The later versions of the adapter ring (14167) and of the multipart ring combination (14158 and 14159) are matched so that measurement has to be carried out also at the working aperture.

You will find further information in the detailed operating instructions for these accessories.

The Leicaflex Motor

Scientific or technological investigations, press and sports photography present many occassions in which a motor-driven camera is desirable for rapid-sequence series of pictures or remote-control shutter release. Even if you take single pictures only you will find the motor drive a valuable aid in many

The motor of the Leicaflex SL MOT can be attached to the camera by a few turns of the wingnut in the bottom. The battery housing is situated on the right and is simply pulled out with a single movement.

64

Leicaflex SL MOT in action — 2 decisive seconds

1970 Football World Championship — final match Brazil vs. Italy in the Aztec Stadium, Mexico City. 72nd minute.

Burgnich (Italy, No. 2) is unable to prevent Pele (Brazil, No. 10) from passing the ball to Jairzinho. Goalkeeper Albertosi realizes the great danger. Jairzinho kicks the ball seemingly into the right corner. Albertosi is deceived, throwing himself on the ground (picture 4). The ball passes him by into the left corner (picture 5). Albertosi swings round (picture 6). Jairzinho follows the ball into the goal (picture 7).

situations; you are continuously ready for action and able to concentrate entirely on the correct moment for releasing the shutter.

For use with the Leicaflex motor a special version of the Leicaflex, the Leicaflex SL MOT, is necessary. The motor can be attached and detached with only a few manipulations.

Whereas for single-frame exposures with automatic shutter wind all speeds from 1 to $1/2000$ sec (except B) can be used, for serial exposures only the speeds from $1/30$ to $1/2000$ sec are suitable, because for the speeds from 1 to $1/15$ sec the motor wind is too fast to leave enough time for the return of the retarding mechanism.

The motor is powered by ten 1.5v midget batteries (R6; U.S.A.: Aa) in a special housing. When inserting them ensure that the + and −symbols in the housing match those on the batteries.

Several types of battery are available in this size. For our purpose, only those delivering a strong current are suitable, such as Pertrix 244, Daimon 298, Ever Ready HP7, Berec HP7, Hellesens 738, Eveready 1015 and E91. Nickel-cadmium batteries with sinter electrodes, such as DEAC 451 RS by Varta A.G., 3 Hannover, are even better for this purpose; they require the Varta charger, Code No. 3261340011, which must be set for charging 10 of these batteries.

At low temperatures all sources of electric power deliver less current. For work in temperatures below −5° C (23° F) the Dryfit Type 6 Sx 3S battery with carrying case and plug manufactured by Accumulatorenfabrik Sonnenschein GmbH, 647 Buedingen, Germany, is most suitable. A charger is available under Code No. 97236 from the same company; Leitz connecting cable with safety switch, Code No. 14175.

Films can be loaded and unloaded with the motor in position. If the motor is to cut out after fewer than 36 exposures, it must be allowed a pre-run without film through as many frames as make up the total of 36. In addition, 2 blank exposures must be allowed for. But the counting mechanism of the motor considers only exposures made with the motor. If the camera was switched for single exposures without motor between motor operations, these exposures will not be recorded. It is therefore possible that the motor can wind only half a frame because the end of the film has been reached. Here, immediate

Removing the battery housing is as simple as this after the unlocking button has been pressed. If a second battery housing is available the energy source can be instantly replaced. It is also possible to prevent a power drop in cold weather if the battery is kept warm in the jacket pocket until it is used.

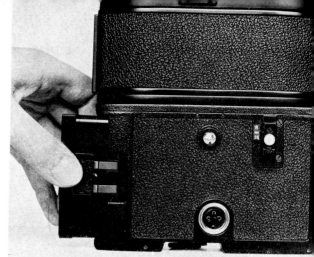

The connecting cable for the remote supply ends in this container, to be inserted in the motor unit in place of the battery housing. During overload the safety switch in the top part of the housing jumps out. The counter is installed at the top, and the three-pole socket for the remote release at the bottom in the back.

This remote release with counter is capable of operating the motorized camera from distances of up to 880yd (800m). The counter records only those exposures that have been made with the motor. The device can be used also in association with a special interval timer for automatic exposure sequences.

rewinding is called for or the battery housing must be pulled out, because at the half-wound position the current remains switched on.

The motor starts only when the winding lever of the camera is in the parked or the measuring position; it will not do so when the lever is swung out. The film counter must be reset when a new film is inserted.

Since the motor is started electrically, any remote release that can be operated by an electric contact can be used. Contacts may be actuated by electric cables, light traps, and pneumatic or hydraulic transmission. A radio remote release is available from B. Kranz, Hamburg 70, Ellerneck 8 through photo dealers. In most countries the operation of radio-controlled remote releases must be authorized by the postal authorities.

To eliminate interference between several releases, the frequency allocation scheme must be set with plug-in crystals. The manufacturers will be pleased to provide further information.

For remote control, both a simple cable with push-button and a new remote release with built-in counter in addition to the remote-release contact is available. This counter reliably records the number of remote-controlled exposures; at the same time it provides functional control by reporting only those exposures which have in fact been made with the motor. The range of the remote releases can be extended by means of extension cables.

A more rapid frame sequence of 6–7fps can be obtained with the Leicaflex SL MOT and a tandem device. This consists of a rail, on which two Leicaflex SL MOT sets are mounted; they are wired so that whilst one camera is being wound the other exposes and vice versa. If both cameras are fitted with lenses of the same focal length, double the number of frames is therefore exposed. It is, however, also possible to use different focal lengths, such as 35mm and 135mm, which record both general aspects and interesting details.

The motors can be operated separately or jointly.

This attachable handle makes
hand-held work easier. The
knurled screw on the foot can
be released and the width of the
loop adjusted to fit the user's
hand. The outfit can thus be
securely gripped in any situation.

This special tripod holder was
designed for setting up the
Leicaflex/motor combination
rigidly on a tripod. The tripod
seating is favourably placed and
permits firm attachment.

Two Leicaflex MOT outfits are
mounted side by side on a
special support rail in the tandem device. The shutter release
is situated in the handgrip.
There is a wide scope for the
tandem device not only in sports
and general reportage, but also
in the scientific and industrial
field.

Technical data of the Leicaflex lenses

Name	Speed	Focal length in mm	Number of elements	Angle of view diagonal	Angle of view horizontal	Angle of view vertical	Click stop apertures	Range of distance settings	Smallest object field in inch	Filter size-Series	Weight in g
Super-Angulon-R*	3,4	21	8	92°	81°	60°	3,4–22	∞–0,2	148×221	VIII	228
Super-Angulon-R**	4	21	10	92°	81°	60°	4 –22	∞–0,2	148×221	VIII₁/₂	445
Elmarit-R	2,8	28	8	76°	65°	46°	2,8–16	∞–0,3	188×282	VII	265
Elmarit-R	2,8	35	7	64°	54°	38°	2,8–22	∞–0,3	140×210	VI	400
Summicron-R	2	35	9	64°	54°	38°	2 –16	∞–0,3	140×210	VII	510
PA-Curtagon	4	35	7	64°	54°	38°	4 –22	∞–0,3	140×210	VIII	300
Summicron-R	2	50	6	45°	38°	26°	2 –16	∞–0,5	180×270	VI	340
Summilux-R	1,4	50	7	45°	38°	26°	1,4–16	∞–0,5	180×270	VII	450
Elmarit-R	2,8	90	5	27°	23°	15°	2,8–22	∞–0,7	140×210	VII	515
Summicron-R	2	90	5	27°	23°	15°	2 –16	∞–0,75	144×216	VII	560
Macro-Elmar	4	100	4	24°	20°	14°	4 –22	bellows	24× 36	VII	380
Elmarit-R	2,8	135	5	18°	15°	10°	2,8–22	∞–1,5	220×330	VII	655
Elmarit-R	2,8	180	5	14°	12°	8°	2,8–16	∞–2	213×320	VIII	1325
Telyt-R	4	250	6	10°	8,5°	6°	4 –22	∞–4,5	368×552	VIII	1380
Telyt-R	6,8	400	2	6°	5°	3,5°	6,8–32	∞–3,5	158×236	VII	1300
Telyt°	5,6	400	2	6°	5°	3,5°	5,6–32	∞–3,6	164×246	VII	2250
Telyt-R	6,8	560	2	4,5°	4°	2,5°	6,8–32	∞–6,4	224×336	VII	2300
Telyt°	5,6	560	2	4,5°	4°	2,5°	5,6–32	∞–6,6	232×348	VII	3260
Telecron-R	6,3	800	3	3°	2,5°	1,5°	6,3–32	∞–12,5	320×480	VII	6850
Angénieux-Zoom	2,8	45/90	15	51/27	44/23	29/15	2,8–16	∞–1	216×324	VIII	780

Key to symbols
  * suitable for use only with brilliant finder (discontinued)
** backfocus type
☐ lens unit only (suitable for use only with the focusing bellows-R))ar).
  ° lenses with Televit-R

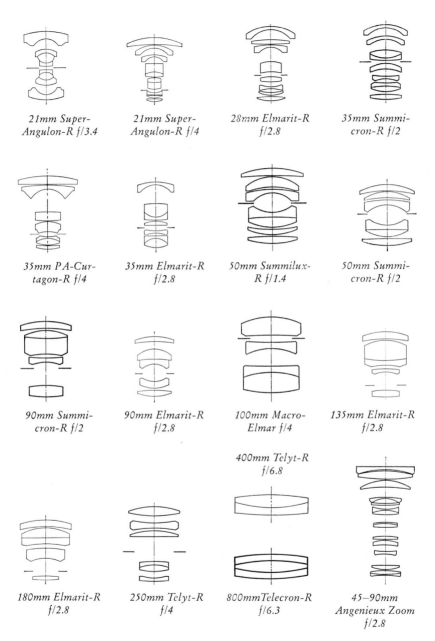

21mm Super-Angulon-R f/3.4

21mm Super-Angulon-R f/4

28mm Elmarit-R f/2.8

35mm Summicron-R f/2

35mm PA-Curtagon-R f/4

35mm Elmarit-R f/2.8

50mm Summilux-R f/1.4

50mm Summicron-R f/2

90mm Summicron-R f/2

90mm Elmarit-R f/2.8

100mm Macro-Elmar f/4

135mm Elmarit-R f/2.8

400mm Telyt-R f/6.8

180mm Elmarit-R f/2.8

250mm Telyt-R f/4

800mm Telecron-R f/6.3

45–90mm Angenieux Zoom f/2.8

The advantages and potentialities of the Leicaflex system

We speak of a system camera if camera body and lens can be easily detached from each other, lenses of various focal lengths are available for interchange, and some accessories for special purposes can be supplied.

The advantages of the 35mm format can be exploited only if the film area is utilized as fully as possible. Enlarging quality suffers if areas of less than 50% of the negative are used. A well graduated scale of focal lengths ensures full utilization of the film format at various camera distances.

The starting point is the standard equipment of the Leicaflex with the 50mm Summicron-R f/2. Since this lens is, with its bayonet mount, quickly interchangeable, you can replace it with lenses of other focal lengths within seconds. The series of lenses begins with the 21mm ultra-wide angle and includes the fast telephoto lens at the other end of the scale.

Your choice of focal length depends on your personal inclination. Often even a single additional focal length is enough to enlarge the range of camera subjects surprisingly. The following recommendations may be adapted to the user's personal preference. In practice, weight, easy handling and focusing range play an important part.

The most versatile additional lens is the 90mm Elmarit-R f/2.8. It occupies pride of place because the advantages especially of this focal length become clearly evident with the single-lens reflex system. But important arguments favour the 135mm Elmarit-R f/2.8 if you prefer to take your photographs from a longer distance; if, on the other hand, panoramic views appeal to you, you will prefer to use a wide-angle lens

Two different effects are obtained through a change in the focal length:

1. better format utilization from a given point of view,

2. changes in the pictorial perspective if with the change of focal length the camera viewpoint is correspondingly changed.

The example of the Augustus Fountain at Augsburg shows clearly how this must be understood. The picture on the left was taken with the 35mm Elmarit-R, the one on the right with the 90mm Elmarit-R. Certainly a wide-angle lens will often be useful, but if you enter the very close-up range at a low camera viewpoint as in this instance, you will find that the perspective foreshortening does not exactly show to advantage. Our bronze Augustus is

not in a position to complain. But if the same thing happened to you in fashion photography, where a low camera viewpoint is also required, the young ladies would soon have something to say about that.

The level of the camera has been left unchanged with the 90mm Elmarit-R. But owing to the longer camera distance the perspective corresponds to that of our normal vision. If you have sufficient freedom of movement and can therefore choose your focal length at will, the use of a 90mm lens will ensure a very natural pictorial rendering.

The advantages of a single-lens reflex camera are noticeable especially with a lens of long focal length and in the close-up range, because the image seen in the viewfinder agrees with that recorded on the film. It is thus possible to utilize the film format from corner to corner. Focusing, too, is the more accur-

73

ate and easy the longer the focal length of the lens in the camera, since the primary magnification of the lens becomes fully effective. The most important interchangeable lenses up to the 180mm Elmarit-R have the large aperture of f/2.8. They are followed by the telephoto lenses of excellent image contrast, of 400mm, 560mm, and 800mm focal length. Their correction is so superb that they can be used at full aperture without hesitation. This offers extremely interesting photographic prospects.

The Elpro achromatic supplementary front lenses open up the close-up range at slight reduction. They improve the optical performance within the close-up range of the lenses for which they are designed. Since the automatic diaphragm control remains fully effective, hand-held photography with these lenses presents no difficulty. Exposure measurement, too, can be carried out normally, because the achromatic front lenses do not produce any appreciable exposure factor.

The lenses for the Leicaflex SL have a second cam, which is adjusted so that the exposure can be measured through the lens at full aperture. This cam transmits to the exposure meter the aperture value intended for the exposure. The other cam is adjusted for the exposure measurement with the earlier model of the Leicaflex. The second cam can be fitted to lenses for the earlier Leicaflex at any time in the factory.

The anti-reflection coating of the Leicaflex lenses

All Leitz lenses have been anti-reflection treated for years with the so-called B-coating, which is vapour-deposited on the lens surface in a high vacuum, and shows a coloured bloom. Whereas the reflecting power of untreated surfaces is in the region of 4–7 %, it is reduced to 1 % and less by the anti-reflection layer which, incidentally, has been found also an effective protection of lenses in the tropics.

The two external surfaces of the lenses are hard-coated for protection against handling. Careful cleaning with a soft sable brush and wiping with lens cleaning tissue does not do any damage.

pp. 75–77: Focal length comparison in the park of Weilburg Castle. All pictures were taken from the same viewpoint. The outlines showing the picture areas covered with the various focal lengths have been entered in the picture taken with the 21mm Super-Angulon-R (top right).

▲ 21 mm   50 mm ▼

▲ 90 mm   250 mm ▼

▲ 400 mm   800 mm ▼

50mm Summicron-R f/2

The 50mm lens is considered the standard equipment for the 35mm format. The single-lens-reflex camera calls for a type of long backfocus (i. e. the distance between the rear member of the lens and the film) so that the movement of the mirror is not obstructed. The 50mm Summicron-R f/2 has therefore been newly computed specially for the Leicaflex.

Its optical performance is superb. The high-precision non-rotating focusing mount allows focusing from ∞ to 0.5m (20in).

This corresponds to an object field of 180 x 270mm at the minimum focusing distance. The adjoining close-up range is opened by the two achromatic front lenses Elpro VIa and VIb (minimum object field 62 x 93mm, see p. 115). When not in use, the lens hood can be inverted on the lens.

50mm Summilux-R f/1.4

This lens is twice as fast as the 50mm Summicron-R f/2. At full aperture it is an excellent reportage lens of brilliant and detail-rich performance. It can be used universally because even when it is stopped down it achieves a general picture quality which is outstanding in the various reproduction ranges. In modern colour photography the use of large apertures offers very attractive possibilities through deliberate restriction of the depth of field.

Its lens hood is of the new design (see illustrations below).

For the attachment of the lens hood the dot must face the pin on the lens. Now push it in the direction of the arrow (1) and turn it towards the right (2).

To remove the lens hood, pull it and turn it towards the right.

50mm Summilux-R f/1.4, ¹/₆₀sec, f/1.4, 400 ASA 27 DIN film.

Photograph by Rudolf Seck

35mm Elmarit-R f/2.8

A wide-angle lens of 35mm focal length and conventional design would so far extend into the Leicaflex as to leave no room for the movement of the hinged miror. But the backfocus construction, which by means of a special optical system reduces the overall length of a telephoto lens to less than what its focal length would ordinarily require, can be used also in wide-angle lenses; conversely, their overall length is increased and — the decisive feature — the distance between the rear element of the lens and the film is considerably longer than the focal length would normally call for. This creates space for the movement of the hinged mirror. One or two large negative elements are used in the front member. This accounts for the fact that in the 35mm Elmarit-R f/2.8 the front lens diameter is larger than in the 50mm Summicron-R f/2. Its optical performance is excellent, a quality which can by no means be taken for granted with backfocus designs. The focusing range extends to 0.3m (12in); the Elpro achromatic front lenses designed for the Summicron-R fit the screw thread of the Elmarit-R, and can be used for threedimensional subjects at apertures of f/11 and smaller. They are less recommended for reproduction, because their optical data have not been computed for backfocus types.

The shorter the focal length of the lens in the camera, the smaller the image of an object in the viewfinder of the Leicaflex; a further typical feature here is that objects in the foreground are rendered "large", and in the background "small". Since the human eye resolves detail only from a certain minimum size upwards, details may be too small to be resolved. Although in practice faulty focusing is not very frequent, nor is it very important at medium and small apertures, you are still advised when using large apertures such as f/4 and f/2.8 to make sure by a quick glance at the focusing scale that the distance set at least approximates the real object distance.

Because of its large angle of view and its large depth of field a 35mm wide-angle lens is eminently suitable for architectural and interior subjects, snapshots and reportage.

City Centre, Frankfurt/M., St. Katharine's Church. 35mm Elmarit-R, f/8, ¹/₁₂₅sec.

Krone's Circus. 35mm Summicron f/2. f/2, ¹/₂₅₀sec.

35mm Summicron f/2

Fast wide-angle lenses of backfocus design are very complicated optical systems. To obtain top performance this lens requires as many as 9 elements. The design of long intercept distance, necessary for single-lens reflex cameras, strongly reduces vignetting (falling off of light towards the corners of the picture with wide-angle lenses at full aperture). This lens is therefore particularly suitable for colour photography even in poor lighting conditions. In spite of the large number of its elements, the pictures it produces are remarkably brilliant. Focusing must be critical for work at full aperture, because the depth of field is, after all, very shallow. The lens hood is attached and removed in the same way as described for the 50mm Summicron-R f/1.4.

In snapshot and reportage work you are often faced with situations in which it is desirable to take the photograph unnoticed. Lifting the camera to the eye already constitutes a risk and may in certain circumstances thwart your photographic intentions completely. The large angle of view of a 35mm wide-angle lens permits exposures without the need to look through the view-finder. On such occassions you will find it very helpful to know the approximate boundaries of your picture area: here is a very useful rule of thumb: The distance to the object approximates the width of the picture.

Since the lens sits rigidly in the camera, it will always point at the centre of the picture. At an object distance of 3m (10ft), for instance, the following picture data will apply: width of picture area 3m (10ft), i. e. extending 1.5m (5ft) each to the left and to the right of the centre of the picture. Height of picture area 2m (6ft 8in), extending 1m (3ft 4in) each upwards and downwards. The following exposure technique is recommended: Determine the shutter speed and lens aperture on a substitute object of similar brightness, and set the estimated distance on the helical focusing mount of the lens. Since the Leicaflex is normally carried on a neck strap or in the ever-ready case in front of the chest, you can aim the lens at the intended centre of the picture without raising the camera to the eye.

35mm PA-Curtagon-R f/4

In architectural and interior photography a correct rendering of the verticals is possible only if the camera is aligned horizontally. Converging verticals caused when the camera is tilted are not due to distortion or any other lens aberration. Care must therefore be taken to avoid tilting the camera when architectural subjects are to be photographed. The resulting empty space in the foreground can be eliminated, for instance with large-format cameras, by a movement of the lens panel.

Pictures with this perspective compensation are now possible also with the Leicaflex. The new 35mm PA-Curtagon f/4 has a considerably larger image circle than is needed for ordinary photography. This reserve makes it possible to displace the lens from the optical axis through up to 7mm in every direction. This principle is of particular value with colour reversal film, where the usual method for the correction of converging verticals cannot be applied. The lens can be displaced in every direction but the four most important positions (towards the top, bottom, left, and right) engage.

Top left: Picture with lens in central position and camera tilted. Bottom left: Camera lined up with the verticals. Empty foreground, top of tower cut off. Top: PA-Curtagon-R displaced upwards through 7mm. Verticals correct, empty foreground removed.

With extreme displacement of the lens from the optical axis f/11 is recommended, unless even smaller stops are called for by the required depth of field. The diaphragm of the PA-Curtagon-R is non-automatic; the shutter speed must therefore be determined with the working aperture. The following method is most suitable for outdoor work in good light: focus your object, stop the lens down to e.g. f/8 or f/11. Adjust the lens paraxially, checking the verticals in the viewfinder. Set the correct shutter speed by rotating the shutter speed dial, release the shutter. For interiors it is preferable to measure at full aperture and to convert the shutter speed for the working aperture used.

85

Dutch Renaissance furniture in the Palais Papius, Museum of European Furniture, Wetzlar. 28mm Elmarit-R f/2.8. f/11, 4sec.   *Photograph by Rudolf Seck*

28mm Elmarit-R f/2.8

This wide-angle lens combines a large angle of view with high speed. Its compact design ensures considerable freedom from vignetting, which is particularly important in colour photography at full aperture. The great depth of field makes it suitable for reportages in confined space and for dynamic advertising photography relying on unusual perspectives. The lens can be used universally at both large and small apertures. Focusing on the focusing screen is practicable only at distances between 1 and 7ft (0.3 and 2m). At longer distances guesswork is quicker and more reliable. This lens is a favourite for interior as well as exterior architectural photography; it has thus a wide range of applications.

21mm Super-Angulon-R f/3.4

The 21mm Super-Angulon-R f/3.4 has the shortest focal length of all Leica-flex lenses. It is supplied in two versions.

At f/3.4 maximum aperture the optical design corresponds to that of the Leica lens of the same designation. It is not a backfocus type, and can therefore be used only in the earlier version of the Leicaflex, in which it is possible to swing the mirror out of the optical path. To do this, turn the preselector lever (3) for the mirror movement downwards. You cannot lock the lens in position as usual by turning it to the right. A small lever, which when the lens is being inserted must rest against the bottom stop, secures the lens as soon as it is pushed up. The lens hoods mounted on each lens also function as retaining rings for filters of Series VIII. No exposure measurement is possible, since the viewfinder window is dark when the mirror is swung out.

The image is viewed by means of a push-on brilliant viewfinder. With close-ups at distances shorter than 1m (40in) the slight parallax resulting from the distance between viewfinder and lens must be allowed for. The viewfinder suffers from slight barrel distortion, which, however, does not occur in the lens.

21mm Super-Angulon-R f/4 (backfocus type)

This lens has an automatic diaphragm, observation of the subject is free from parallax via the mirror of the Leicaflex. The exposure, too, is measured through the lens as usual.

The short-focal-length lens forms a very small image of the details on the focusing screen. This makes focusing difficult because the depth of field is very large, estimation is, however, accurate enough between 1m (40in) and infinity. Distances of less than 1m (40in) should be measured. The film plane (rear end of accessory shoe) is the reference plane. Here, too, the lens hood functions as a retaining ring for the filters, Series VIII^1/$_2$. It is detached by means of a new method: pull it forward and detach the front part by slightly turning it to the left.

Although the depth of field of extremely short-focal-length lenses is very great, the lens should be stopped down further than the depth-of-field scale indicates if the utmost definition is required. The scale is based on a circle of permissible confusion of 1/30mm, but 1/60mm is better still; you will obtain this value by reading the depth of field off the scale at two aperture values larger than set on the lens; for instance, stop down to f/8 and see how far your depth of field extends at f/4. This method is useful because the full pictorial effect of Super-Angulon pictures is revealed only by strong enlargement.

Before you insert the lens in the camera, ensure that the external surface of the rear member is spotlessly clean. A fingermark is quite enough to impair optical performance considerably. Bits of fluff and other impurities are revealed as objectionable patches. At small apertures particles of dirt even on the filter are disturbing owing to the enormous depth of field of the lens. Polarizing filters cannot be used, because only part of the polarized light is extinguished owing to the wide angle of field of the lens.

The unusual properties of the Super-Angulon, its extremely wide angle of view, its extraordinarily great depth of field, and its focusing range down to 20cm (8in) create many possibilities which are out of the question with lenses of longer focal lengths. Pictures of architect's models deserve special emphasis because here the strong perspective foreshortening is pictorially very effective.

Opportunities also abound in industrial and advertising photography. But pictures taken in the belief that the great depth of field allows a snap-

In a car factory. The extreme depth of field necessary here is provided by the 21mm Super-Angulon-R. *Photograph by Rudolf Seck*

shot technique are unsatisfactory unless the full format is utilized. Part enlargements are not very satisfactory in this particular case, and pictures taken with frame-filling focal-length lenses are of much better quality.

It is astonishing that in spite of its extreme angle of view the Super-Angulon hardly suffers from vignetting so that it can be recommended for colour photography without hesitation. If you want your picture to be free from converging verticals you must align the camera vertically and horizontally with even greater care than when you use the 35mm Elmarit-R. Another phenomenon must be considered. According to the laws of central projection spherical objects along the edges of the picture format are reproduced as ellipsoids in the case of extremely wide angles of view.

90mm Elmarit-R f/2.8

Whereas the 35mm and 50mm Leicaflex lenses have been designed so that the location of the nearest lens element allows for unobstructed mirror movement, the opposite method has been adopted with the 90mm Elmarit-R, which is designed like a telephoto lens. The general correction is excellent, and the lens produces corner-to-corner sharpness even at full aperture. Test exposures prove this. But do not use objects in the close-up range for such tests, because camera lenses are corrected for infinity. If they are used for shorter distances their performance is by no means as excellent as at ∞, although it is still satisfactory for ordinary purposes. Here, too, optical quality is improved for close-up subjects by the use of the Elpro VIIa achromatic front lens. Exposure factors are small enough to be ignored.

From a pictorial point of view, the range of the 90mm focal length is the most universal, representing an ideal compromise. It compels you to concentrate the pictorial elements; the various features do not appear to be excessively spaced out, because the depth of field is considerably shallower than with the shorter focal lengths. Operation and weight are so convenient that

This is the model of an industrial plant. Here, too, the 21mm Super-Angulon-R is the only lens which produces a perspective similar to that of a picture of the final original. The figure in the right middle distance in reality measures 9cm (3³/₄in).

Photograph by Rudolf Seck

the danger of camera shake is not increased by the longer focal length. As the objects are viewed at 1.5 x magnification, focusing takes very little time. In the close-up range, operational readiness can be improved by means of the following method: Set a desired distance on the focusing ring, and sway backwards and forwards with the Leicaflex until optimum sharpness is obtained on the focusing screen. This is very quickly learned with a little practice. The following technique is used for snapshots when you want to take advantage of the moment of surprise: let your viewpoint be the apex of an isosceles triangle. Let one side be the measuring distance, the second the distance to the camera subject. By slightly changing the distances obtain a viewpoint equidistant from both points; for your judgement will be excellent if you have distances that are comparable. Observe the scene unobtrusively until the right moment has arrived, wheel round, and release the shutter. After some trial films you will master the technique, which can naturally be used also with other focal lengths. The 90mm lens is particularly recommended for portraiture.

90mm Summicron-R f/2

Because it is a true telephoto lens, at only 62mm its total mechanical length is remarkably short. Its high speed opens up many possibilities even in poor lighting conditions. The shallow depth of field in the close-up range produces interesting effects especially in colour photography. The focusing range is the same as that of the 90mm Elmarit. At the minimum focusing distance of 28in (70cm) it covers an object field of about 6 x 8¹/₂in (144 x 216mm), which makes it a universal lens also in the medium close-up range. With the Elpro VIIa close-up front lens the close-up range is extended down to an object field of 3 x 4¹/₂in (74 x 112mm) (reproduction scale 1:3). In the close-up range it is desirable, indeed customary if only in the interest of depth of field, to stop down to f/5.6 to f/8. The lens hood is extensible as in the 90mm and 135mm Elmarit-R lenses. The 90mm Summicron-R weighs only a little more than the 90mm Elmarit-R f/2.8.

Mikkel, from the settlement of Isortog, is a member of the generation of those East Greenlanders who cannot give their age with certainty. 90mm Elmarit-R.
Photograph by H. Gsellmann

The 90mm Elmarit-R is a versatile lens for circus subjects. Spotlight illumination can give faulty exposure readings. The floor of the ring rather than the subject itself is therefore measured, because the unlit background portions would produce too long an exposure time.

Of this beautiful equestrian act two successful shots were obtained, showing almost the same figure, once from the front, once from the side. We are also including the less favourable aspect to emphasize the importance of the correct viewpoint. Both pictures f/2.8, 1/250sec, 160 ASA (23 DIN).

Even today many an important visitor to Rothenburg ob der Tauber is received with music and offered a deep draught from Mayor Nusch's huge tankard. This type of reportage is easiest with the 90mm Elmarit-R, because the distance to the marching band and the group at the entrance of the Town Hall can be much longer than with the standard-focal-length lens. Since the narrower angle of view also includes less background, pictorial composition is often easier than with lenses of shorter focal lengths.

Both photographs f/8, $^1/_{250}$sec, 160 ASA (23 DIN) film.

135mm Elmarit-R f/2.8

This lens, too, is of telephoto design, and has 5 elements. It owes its excellent optical performance partly to the use of highly refractive glasses. Its resolving power is superb even at full aperture. The main reason for stopping down is to increase the depth of field, which is very limited with such a long focal length. The helical-focusing range has been limited to 1.5m (5ft) in the interest of the highest possible mechanical stability. Shorter focusing distances are feasible with the Elpro VIIb and shorter distances still with the Elpro VIIa achromatic front lens (p. 115).

Focusing on the focusing screen of the Leicaflex SL is amazingly quick and reliable, because the subject is observed at 2.3 x magnification. The high speed and long focal length of the 135mm Elmarit-R are responsible for its considerable weight of 1 lb 7 oz (655 g). But owing to its compact form it fits so snugly on the Leicaflex that we can practically call this combination an integrated whole. Its heavy weight may be inconvenient to carry, but in photography it is no disadvantage, because the ratio of moving parts (shutter and mirror) to inert mass becomes more favourable.

The filter diameter, Size VII, is the same as for the 90mm Elmarit-R. The lens hood is extensible like a telescope.

Because of its narrow angle of field the 135mm focal length often allows the photographer to work at a suitable distance from his subject. Fenced-off sports contests or reportages of official events can be covered by the camera only if the long distance can be bridged by the use of a long focal length.

Not only the 90mm lenses, but also the 135mm Elmarit can be used as a portrait lens with outstanding results. The camera distance is increased by half, which is often most convenient; so is the shallow depth of field, which suppresses the background even more strongly than with the 90mm lenses.

Figure on the Augustus Fountain, Augsburg. 135mm. Elmarit-R, f/11, 1/125sec.

180mm Elmarit-R f/2.8

A telephoto lens of this speed and focal length extends the photographic possibilities quite considerably. Although its weight is appreciable, it is not at all disturbing during the exposure, because heavy weights can be held more steadily. The optical performance is excellent. The lens is a 5-element telephoto system of outstanding resolving power and flatness of field.

The lens hood is built on to the lens mount and extended for use. The iris diaphragm has click stops also for intermediate values; the minimum aperture is f/16. The focusing range extends from infinity to 6ft 8in (2m). At the minimum distance the picture area measures 9 x 13in approx. (22 x 33cm). The larger the deviation from the standard focal length the more unusual the pictures that can be produced with such a lens. But we must not conceal the fact that the exposure technique here calls for more experience and practice.

Left: The 180mm Elmarit-R is a telephoto lens. The diagram on page 71 shows details of its optical design.

Right: Fig tree on the coast of Southern Portugal. 180mm Elmarit-R, f/2.8, f/8, ¹/₂₅₀*sec.* *Photograph by Julius Behnke*

98

250mm Telyt-R f/4

From its outward appearance this lens could almost be confused with the 180mm Elmarit-R. It has the same diameter, almost the same weight, and is less than 1in (2cm) longer. This was achieved with a mechanical length that is remarkably short for a telephoto lens system, and by the reduction of the aperture by one stop. Handling the 250mm Telyt-R is also similar in many respects to that of the 180mm Elmarit-R. The high magnification and the good contrast rendering of the Leicaflex viewfinder ensure accurate and reliable focusing.

Event at full aperture the optical performance of this lens is excellent across the entire field. Stopping down is necessary only to increase the depth of field or for close-up subjects. The combination drawing shows that the various elements are comparatively thin. Nevertheless, the combination of long focal length, high lens speed, and the necessary robust mount results in a weight of 3lb 1oz (1380g).

At such a long focal length the depth of field is very shallow, so that the critically focused object stands out quite clearly against the unsharp background.

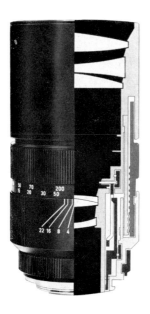

Left: Fully automatic spring-back diaphragm. Stop values (click-stops also for half values) f/4 − f/22. Focusing range ∞ − 15ft (4.5m). Filter series VII. Extensible lens hood.

Right: Park of Weilburg Castle. 250mm Telyt-R f/4, f/5.6, ¹/₂₅₀sec, 32 ASA (16 DIN) film.

45–90mm Angénieux Zoom f/2.8

This is a zoom lens for the Leicaflex by the well-known Paris firm of Angénieux. The diaphragm control of the mount is matched with that of the other Leicaflex lenses, i. e. the lens has an automatic spring-back diaphragm with stop values (click-stops also for half values) f/2.8–f/22. As in the conventional Leicaflex lenses, the exposure is measured at full aperture. The zoom range is continuous from 45mm to 90mm focal length. The plane of sharpness is preserved even when the focal length is changed.

As in all zoom lenses the optical design is rather complicated. The lens consists of 15 elements in 12 members. The loss of light owing to absorption and reflection in so many elements is automatically allowed for in the exposure measurement. The most important advantage of such a type of lens is that it allows a precise utilization of the film format within its range of focal lengths, of interest especially when colour reversal film is used. The colour rendering is a trifle warmer than that of all the other Leicaflex lenses, which makes the use of an additional U. V. filter unnecessary.

Right: Frickenhausen on Main. The top picture was taken at the 45mm, the bottom picture at the 90mm setting. Although the range of variation extends to only twice the minimum focal length, only a quarter of the picture area is covered. If all the intermediate settings are considered, the possibilities of pictorial composition are numerous.

The Televit-R rapid focusing device

Long and ultra-long focal lengths demand parallax-free observation and critical focusing. The new focusing screen of the Leicaflex SL is particularly well suited for long focal lengths because focusing is possible not only inside the inner circle, but also on the microscreen of the surrounding field. Exposure measurement through the lens, too, offers real advantages. The Televit-R should therefore be used on the Leicaflex SL only.

The rapid focusing device consists of the focusing unit — a movable sturdy length of tube with a hand-grip — and the diaphragm tube, into which the 400mm or 560mm Telyt f/5.6 lenses are screwed. By means of an adapter ring the lens unit of the 280mm Telyt f/4.8, too, can be used on the focusing unit.

Focusing should be a rapid, yet delicate operation. This is an old wish that has been realized in the Televit-R. The lock for the coarse focusing is released by means of a plunger in the hand-grip, and the Leicaflex body can be easily moved relative to the hand-grip. The focusing position is locked as soon as the plunger is released. The fine focusing is adjusted by means of a rubberized rotating knob. Without tripod, the Televit-R is operated as follows:

Grip the hand-grip with your left hand, placing the thumb on the rotating knob. When you have completed the coarse focusing by moving the camera back or forwards, release the plunger; you can now carry out the fine focusing with the thumb on the rotating knob. Your right hand grips the Leicaflex with the index finger resting on the release button. In an elongated slot on the left of the focusing device you will find two adjustable screws. If you wish, you can use them as limiting stops for two distances (near and far point); you can, however, focus any intermediate distance at will.

The diaphragm of the lenses used in the Televit is of the preset, not the automatic, type. With very large lens diameters the structural problems of the automatic diaphragm are very difficult to solve. But since with practice it is possible to focus down to f/11 in average lighting conditions the situations in which the automatic diaphragm will be missed are few and far between. For focusing the microscreen of the surrounding field instead of the central field is used.

The rapid focusing device is adjusted in the factory so that the lenses can be focused slightly beyond their infinity position. If you want to use an infinity stop in certain situations, you can set this with the front stop screw for the distance limitation.

In the Leicaflex SL the exposure is measured at the working aperture. The advantages resulting from the high light transmission of the achromats (only two glass-air boundaries) are automatically allowed for.

At the 60mm focusing travel of the Televit-R the various lenses have the following focusing ranges:

			m	ft in	Minimum picture area
280mm	f/5.6	∞	— approx. 2.2	7'3"	134 x 201mm
400mm	f/5.6	∞	— approx. 3.6	11'10"	164 x 246mm
560mm	f/5.6	∞	— approx. 6.6	21'8"	232 x 348mm

To make hand-held operation easier a stock is included in the outfit. Nevertheless, the lens hood should also be supported or proped up if this is at all possible. If you work with the camera hand-held and use a neck strap (14130), this should be attached to the Televit-R or to the diaphragm tube, not to the Leicaflex.

Series VII filters can be inserted in a swing-out filter holder. This has advantages in work with colour, because the delicately graded correction filters, almost unobtainable in the diameters of the lens units, can now be used. Focusing must be carried out with the filter in position.

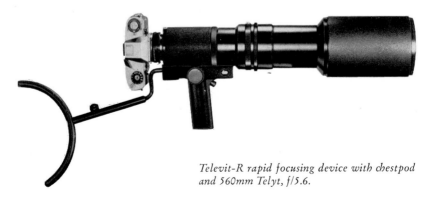

Televit-R rapid focusing device with chestpod and 560mm Telyt, f/5.6.

The 400mm and 560mm Telyt-R f/6.8 rapid-action lenses

The wish to be able to take photographs almost as quickly with long- as with medium-focal-length lenses has led to the development of these special lens designs. To achieve this, a completely new procedure of focusing was essential and the solution found is eminently successful. The focusing mechanism is released by pressure on a button; the front part with the lens mount can now be accurately yet most easily adjusted. The very long focal lengths reveal instantly when an object is in critical focus on the focusing screen of the Leicaflex. Focusing must, however, be carried out in the field surrounding the measuring wedge, because the screen of the latter is slightly darkened at f/6.8.

The lens is an achromat of excellent correction and, naturally, is anti-reflection coated; the picture contrast is very high. The lens consists of two cemented elements, so that it has only two glass-air interfaces; this results in the best possible light transmission and brilliance. Exposure, too, is less than with a multi-element lens of the same aperture because losses of light caused by absorption in the glasses and by reflection on the surfaces cannot occur. Contrast plays an important part in subjects at long distances because the slight atmospheric haze almost always veiling such subjects cuts down picture contrast. The high brilliance of the Leicaflex viewfinder image not only affects image quality; it also facilitates focusing.

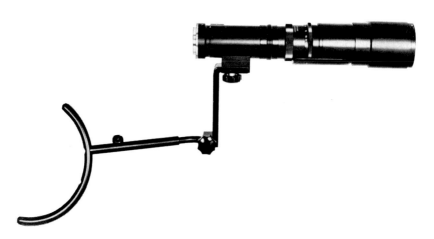

Slalom training. 400mm Telyt-R, f/8, yellow filter, ¹/₅₀₀sec.

Photograph by Prof. S. Kruckenhauser

A considerable advantage of the new focusing method is also the long displacement range of 60mm. In association with the 400mm focal length this produces a focusing range from ∞ to 12ft (3.6m) and with the 560mm focal length from ∞ to 21ft 4in (6.4m). For transport the lens units with the focusing mounts and the lens tubes can be separated. An extension tube (length 60mm, Code No. 14182) can be inserted for close-up photography, increasing the focusing range of the 400mm lens from 12ft (3.6m) to 7ft 8in (2.3m) and providing a smallest object field of 3.2 x 4.8in (80 x 120mm). For the 560mm lens the focusing range is increased from 21ft 4in (6.4m) to 13ft 4in (4m); the smallest object field is 4.8 x 7.2in (120 x 180mm).

A slot built into the lens tube accommodates Series VII filters. The light-screening device for this slot is removed by withdrawal in the direction of the camera. When released it springs back into the screening position. During the use of filters the object must be focused with the filters in position, since the filter is in the rear optical path. Only optically flawless filters are suitable.

The lens diaphragms have clickstops (also for half values), but are not automatic and have no presetting facilities. Depending on the lighting conditions focusing is easy at f/8 or, if the light is bright, even at f/11, making a diaphragm control mechanism unnecessary.

Since the rapid-action lenses are often used without tripod they are supplied with shoulder stocks. The 400mm lens can be conveniently hand held with it, since its total weight is only 4lb (1800g). With the 560mm lens it is very useful to prop the leather-covered lens hood up on some additional support. The total weight of this outfit is 5lb 2oz (2300g).

800mm Telecron-R f/6.3

Telephoto lenses of extremely long focal lengths present the optical computer with a difficult task. As the focal length increases, the residual chromatic aberrations become more and more prominent. In the past, only crystal glass was available as a means of correction. But this suffers from the weakness of insufficient chemical and physical stability and is therefore not very suitable for the manufacture of large lenses.

The glass research laboratories of Messrs. Leitz have, after prolonged trials, succeeded in the development of glasses whose extreme optical data closely approximate those of crystal glass without sharing its disturbing faults. It has been possible with the aid of one of these special glasses to compute an achromatic triplet of a hitherto unequalled optical performance. Its correction borders on the apochromatic. The residual unsharpness has been reduced to less than one third of the values of conventional types of glass. This goes hand in hand with an increase in contrast, detail resolution, and colour differentiation. The lens consists of three cemented elements and presents only two glass-air interfaces. The light transmission of the system is consequently very high.

The lens is stopped down with an ordinary iris diaphragm, which offers all the advantages of increased depth of field. It is a well-known fact that conventional stopping down is not possible with reflecting lenses. The focusing range extends from ∞ to 41ft 8in (12.5m). A slot accommodates Series VII filters. As the lens weighs 15lb 4oz (6860g), it can be used only with a sturdy tripod. For the photography of stationary objects an additional tripod support can be fixed to the lens hood. For transport the lens can be dismantled into three parts.

Lenses of extremely long focal lengths produce a peculiar perspective, in which even widely separated objects move comparatively close together in the picture. This unusual presentation is very popular with experienced photographers as a means of pictorial composition. Since considerable progress has been made in increasing the resolving power of ultra-fast films, these films are to be preferred. They allow fast shutter speeds, which are the safest protection against movement blur in the picture.

Three-part ring combination for photography at the reproduction scales 1:2 and 1:1 with the 50mm Summicron-R f/2

The combination consists of three different rings screwed together as shown in the illustration below. The two outer rings have a bayonet fitting for the camera and for the lens respectively. Together they are 25mm high; the middle ring has the same height, and as many middle rings as required can be used. Some variations are listed in the table on p. 112. The combination is suitable not only for the 50mm and 90mm lenses, but, as camera extension, also for other focal lengths.

The earlier version 14134-1 and 14134-2 has now been superseded by the combination 14158-1 and 14158-2, which includes a semi-automatic spring-back diaphragm. For focusing, the lens diaphragm can be arrested in the open position. Pressure on a button or a twin cable release stops the lens diaphragm down to the preset value immediately before the shutter is released. The new combination thus speeds up the operation of the Leicaflex.

The exposure factors listed in the table should be considered only when the first version of the Leicaflex, which does not yet feature through-the-lens exposure measurement, is used. In the Leicaflex SL the exposure must be

New version of the ring combination with semi-automatic springback diaphragm.

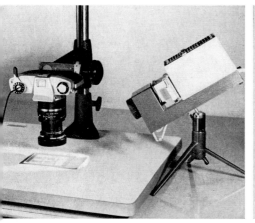

For the picture of this postage stamp the Leicaflex SL with the 50mm Summicron-R f/2 with the ring combination 14134 and the Elpro VIb achromatic front lens was used on the copying stand 16707, which is eminently suitable for this purpose because the large knob on the column makes focusing easy. The Pradix projector, which has a tripod bush on its underside, was used as a light source. It should not be habitually placed at as steep an angle as shown in the illustration, because the projector lamp is designed for upright use. It would have been better if the stamp had been set up about 3¹/₄in (8cm) higher, when the projector would have been almost horizontal, and its light almost glancing across the surface (important with relief-print).

measured at the working aperture. If the light is too weak for this, the exposure can be measured at full aperture, but the shutter speed must be converted for the working aperture. If the aperture is so small that the central screen becomes dark, the object must be focused on the micro-screen of the surrounding field.

Owners of Elpro close-up front lenses will find that these improve picture quality. It is recommended always to stop down to f/8 and even further if circumstances permit.

An earlier version of 14134-2 (without * in front of the Code-No.) does not yet include a limit stop so that the exposure with the Leicaflex SL can be measured at the working aperture; here the film speed must be reduced by 2 DIN (0.64x ASA value) as correction.

* 14134 corresponds to 14158 of the new version with semi-automatic spring-back diaphragm.

Three-part adapter ring for the LEICAFLE

Combinations	Distance scale		Object-film distance	
	m	inch	mm	inch
*14134-1+14134-2	∞	∞	231	9.09'
14134-1+14134-2	0.5	20"	215	8.46'
14134-1+14134-2+ELPRO VIa	∞	∞	212	8.35'
14134-1+14134-2+ELPRO VIa	0.5	20"	203	8.03'
14134-1+14134-2+ELPRO VIb	∞	∞	196	7.72'
14134-1+14134-2+ELPRO VIb	0.5	20"	192	7.56'
14134-1+14135+14134-2	∞	∞	202	7.95'
14134-1+14135+14134-2	1.5	60"	202	7.95'
14134-1+14135+14134-2	0.5	20"	203	7.99'
14134-1+14135+14134-2+ELPRO VIa	∞	∞	199	7.83'
14134-1+14135+14134-2+ELPRO VIa	0.5	20"	201	7.91'
14134-1+14135+14134-2+ELPRO VIb	∞	∞	194	7.64'
14134-1+14135+14135-2+ELPRO VIb	0.5	20"	197	7.72'

Three-part adapter ring for the LEICAFL

Combinations	Distance scale		Object-film distance	
*14134-1+14134-2	∞	∞	512	20.16'
14134-1+14134-2	0.7	28"	403	15.94'
14134-1+14134-2+ELPRO VIIa	∞	∞	383	15.08'
14134-1+14134-2+ELPRO VIIa	0.7	28"	342	13.50'
14134-1+14135+14134-2	∞	∞	375	14.76'
14134-1+14135+14134-2	0.7	28"	352	13,86'
14134-1+14135+14134-2+ELPRO VIIa	∞	∞	331	13.03'
14134-1+14135+14134-2+ELPRO VIIa	0.7	28"	323	12.72'
14134-1+14135+14135+14134-2	∞	∞	346	13.62'
14134-1+14135+14135+14134-2	0.7	28"	343	13.50'
14134-1+14135+14135+14134-2+ELPRO VIIa	∞	∞	323	12.72'
14134-1+14135+14135+14134-2+ELPRO VIIa	0.7	28"	326	12.83'

m Summicron-R f/2

| ct-front lens distance | Object size | | Repro-duction scale | Depth of field circle of confusion = $^1/_{30}$ mm at f/11 | | Extension factor* |
inch	mm	inch		mm	inch	
5.31"	49.9 × 74.9	1.96 × 2.95"	1:2.08	4.5	0.18"	2.0
4.41"	39.1 × 58.7	1.55 × 2.32"	1:1.63	3.0	0.12"	2.4
3.70"	39.4 × 59.0	1.55 × 2.32"	1:1.64	2.8	0.11"	2.0
3.15"	32.4 × 48.6	1.28 × 1.91	1:1.35	2.1	0.08"	2.4
3.03"	32.4 × 48.6	1.28 × 1.91"	1:1.35	1.9	0.07"	2.0
2.64"	27.4 × 41.0	1.08 × 1.61"	1:1.14	1.5	0.06"	2.4
3.19"	25.0 × 37.4	0.98 × 1.47"	1:1.04	1.5	0.06"	3.5
3.11"	24.0 × 36.0	0.94 × 1.42"	1:1.00	1.4	0.055"	3.6
2.95"	22.0 × 33.0	0.87 × 1.30"	1.09:1	1.2	0.05"	3.9
2.24"	22.0 × 33.0	0.87 × 1.30"	1.09:1	1.2	0.045"	3.5
2.05"	19.7 × 29.5	0.78 × 1.16"	1.22:1	1.0	0.038"	3.9
1.97"	19.5 × 29.3	0.77 × 1.15"	1.23:1	0.9	0.035"	3.5
1.81"	17.6 × 26.5	0.69 × 1.04 "	1.36:1	0.8	0.031"	3.9

mm Elmarit-R f/2.8

	inch	mm	inch	Repro-duction scale	mm	inch	Extension factor*
	14.80"	86.4 × 129.6	3.40 × 5.10	1:3.60	12.4	0.49"	1.7
2	10.00"	53.5 × 79.9	2.12 × 3.17	1:2.22	5.4	0.22"	2.2
2	9.13"	54.5 × 81.7	2.15 × 3.22"	1:2.27	4.9	0.19"	1.7
	6.93"	38.6 × 58.0	1.53 × 2.30"	1:1.61	2.8	0.11"	2.2
4	8.42"	43.2 × 64.8	1.70 × 2.55"	1:1.80	3.8	0.15"	2.6
6	6.97"	32.9 × 49.3	1.30 × 1.96"	1:1.37	2.5	0.10"	3.2
5	6.10"	32.6 × 49.0	1.28 × 1.93"	1:1.36	2.2	0.09"	2.6
2	5.20"	26.2 × 39.2	1.04 × 1.56"	1:1.09	1.6	0.063"	3.2
	6.30"	28.8 × 43.2	1.13 × 1.70"	1:1.20	2.0	0.08"	3.7
2	5.59"	24.0 × 36.0	0.94 × 1.42"	1:1	1.5	0.061"	4.4
2	4.80"	23.3 × 35.0	0.92 × 1.98"	1.03:1	1.3	0.053"	3.7
9	4.29"	19.8 × 29.8	0.79 × 1.18"	1.21:1	1.1	0.042"	4.4

the Leicaflex SL the exposure factors are automatically included in the measurement if this is
en at the working aperture.

Elpro achromatic front lens attachments for close-up photography

The Elpro achromatic front lenses (originally called Makrotar) consist of two cemented elements specially computed for use in the close-up range. They therefore not only extend the focusing range, but also improve the optical quality of the picture.

They offer further advantages: the automatic diaphragm mechanism remains fully operative; no extension factors need be allowed for the exposure, because even in the most unfavourable conditions they remain so small that they can be ignored.

The focal lengths of the Elpro close-up lenses are matched so that their range is continuous with that of the helical focusing mount of the lens and of other Elpro lenses. The Roman numerals denote their diameters. The Elpros VIa and VIb are designed for use on the 50mm Summicron-R f/2. The Elpro VIIa can be used on both the 90mm and the 135mm Elmarit-R f/2.8, whereas the use of the Elpro VIIb is confined to the 135mm Elmarit-R f/2.8. The table on p. 115 lists the focusing ranges, reproduction scales, and object field sizes. The focal lengths of the various Elpro achromatic front lenses will also be found there. P. 180 contains directions and hints for the camera technique in the close-up range.

The 100mm Macro-Elmar f/4 can be combined with the Elpro VIIa. Further details are discussed under "Focusing Bellows-R".

First, unscrew the filter retaining ring on the Leicaflex lens; replace it with the Elpro close-up lens. The front thread of this lens is the same as that of the camera lens, and the filter retaining ring can also be screwed in here. Filters and lens hoods are handled as on the camera lens.

Focusing table for the Elpro achromatic front lenses

Further possibilities of use exist besides the combinations already described, either with the 35mm Elmarit-R f/2.8 or as a combination of 2 Elpro close-up lenses. Although possible, these combinations are not recommended because they do not improve the optical performance of the system. You are advised to stop down to f/11 or f/16 should you find the use of these combinations essential.

If the depth-of-field values for f/5.6 are required the values for f/11 must be halved. For the 90mm and 135mm Elmarits the values for f/22 are obtained if those for f/11 are doubled.

The values listed in the table for the 90mm Elmarit-R f/2.8 apply also to the 90mm Summicron f/2.

Leicaflex lens	ELPRO	Distance scale at	Distance Object to Film	Size of Object field in inch	Reproduction scale	Depth of field in inch		
						8	11	16
50 mm SUMMICRON-R f/2	VIa	∞	20"	7.25 × 10.88	1:7.7	1.4	2	2.8
	VIa	20"	12"	3.58 × 5.37	1:3.8	0.4	0.56	0.8
	VIb	∞	12"	3.70 × 5.55	1:3.9	0.4	0.56	0.8
	VIb	20"	9.5"	2.44 × 3.66	1:2.6	0.2	0.28	0.4
90 mm ELMARIT-R f/2.8	VIIa	∞	29"	6.34 × 9.51	1:6.7	1	1.4	2
	VIIa	28"	17.3"	2.87 × 4.31	1:3	0.25	0.35	0.5
135 mm ELMARIT-R f/2.8	VIIb	∞	5'	9.33 × 14	1:9.9	2.3	3.2	4.6
	VIIb	5'	33.5"	4.21 × 6.32	1:4.5	0.5	0.7	1
	VIIa	∞	30"	4.21 × 6.32	1:4.5	0.5	0.7	1
	VIIa	5'	23"	2.60 × 3.9	1:2.8	0.22	0.31	0.44

Focusing bellows for the Leicaflex SL

The new focusing bellows has been designed mainly with the Leicaflex SL in mind. Its high-precision and robust construction meets all the requirements of rapid and reliable operation. The long extension of 100mm, which can be adjusted continuously, of this bellows unit enlarges the photographic range of the camera in many respects. The focusing bellows is indispensable especially in the scientific sector, and with close-up- and macrophotography.

The front panel of the bellows has the same bayonet mount as the Leicaflex SL. All Leicaflex lenses from 50mm to 180mm focal length can be inserted. But because of their automatic diaphragms and automatic exposure control, the lens units can no longer be unscrewed from their mounts. If the lenses are used on the focusing bellows, the infinity setting cannot be obtained, because their extension is increased by 42mm owing to the thickness of the bellows and the bayonet mounts. In practice this means that these lenses can be used on the focusing bellows in the close-up range only.

To cover the range from ∞ to 1:1 a special lens has therefore been designed, the 100mm Macro-Elmar f/4.* Its correction is excellent, and its performance range includes the close-up distances. The automatic diaphragm mechanism of the Leicaflex has been modified so that alternatively manual diaphragm adjustment or mechanical springback diaphragm operation by means of a twin-cable release is possible. Series VII filters can be used on the Macro-Elmar and the Elpro VIIa achromatic front lens can therefore also be screwed in, offering a reproduction range from 1:7 to 1.3:1.

The adapter 14167 can be mounted in the front bayonet of the universal focusing bellows.The following Leica lenses can be used with it: 65mm Elmar f/3.5, 90mm Elmarit f/2.8 lens unit, and 135mm Tele-Elmar f/4 lens unit. The diaphragms of these lenses must always be adjusted by hand.

The image is focused by means of the large knurled knob on the left. To open the diaphragm at the same time, laterally press against the sprung disc lying against the knurled knob. When this is released the diaphragm is closed to the preset value. If you wish to use the springback diaphragm, arrest the open diaphragm by means of a small lock.

A rotating bar with scales is located below the setting knob; here the reproduction scales for the 100mm Macro-Elmar and the 90mm and 135mm

---

* to be used in the focusing bellows only.

Elmarit-R lenses can be read; the fourth scale indicates the extension of the bellows in mm. All you have to do if you want to repeat an exposure at a certain reproduction scale is read the value off this mm-scale and set it again when required; for focusing, move the entire bellows unit backwards or forwards.

The exposure time is measured at the working aperture. Extension factors are no longer operative with the exposure measurement for close-up subjects with the Leicaflex SL, since the increase in the camera extension is automatically allowed for. But when the focusing bellows is used with the earlier Leica-flex, extension factors must be applied. Note the reproduction scales on the rotating scale bar.

To allow a lens to be focused in the close-up range without a change in the reproduction scale the focusing bellows has an additional rack-and-pinion movement on the underside of the tripod slide; this provides the fine adjustment after the total distance has been roughly determined. The lower drive knob is arrested by means of a wing nut.

With high shutter speeds you can work with the assembly handheld, but on the whole a sturdy tripod with a solid ball-and-socket head is to be preferred. The tripod bush is located in the underside of the fine-adjustment drive.

The advantages of the 35mm format

The 35mm (24 x 36mm) format represents a compromise, but a favourable one. It is so small and inexpensive and the 35mm equipment weighs so little that you can shoot your pictures without inhibitions. It does not matter if you take the same subject from four different points of view, if with moving subjects you try a dozen times to find the best solution, and if you use three different exposure times in extreme lighting conditions.

When you are planning a journey, not to mention an expedition, you have to calculate everything in advance. Weight, volume and price of the equipment must be tolerable. Who know beforehand whether he should be prepared for 350 or for 700 pictures? Ten 135-36 colour films weigh 1 lb (450g); ordinary black-and-white material only 9oz (250g). You need therefore not worry about weight; as far as cost is concerned, too, the 35mm film is the most reasonable.

The small format does, however, demand perfect exposure technique and firstclass equipment. The latter condition is met by the Leicaflex with its superb lenses. The opinion that quality is increased by a larger format is biassed unless you consider all the factors involved.

A close relationship exists between lens speed, focal length and camera format For the 35mm format a much better correction is possible for high lens speeds; plane position of the film in the camera is also much more easily ensured with the small format. The comparison becomes clear and "weighty" if you correlate the interchangeable lenses of the Leicaflex with their opposites for the 6 x 9cm (2¹/₄ x 3¹/₄in) format. The following focal lengths are equivalent:

24 x 36mm	21	35	50	90	135	180mm
60 x 90mm	53	88	125	225	338	450mm

You will never fail to be surprised when you see lenses of these equivalent focal lengths side by side in the original. Expense increases considerably with increasing camera formats. Operational and other related aspects, too, change accordingly; the exposure technique especially for moving subjects becomes difficult.

The sum of the advantages of the 35mm format is large. There are obvious instances in which a far larger format is much more efficient, such as pure architecture, when the convergence of verticals must be prevented already at the exposure stage, and astrophotography, where only the planeness of a glass plate is acceptable. The 35mm format represents a compromise; but it is a compromise that has its advantages.

How sharp can a picture be?

When you look at a $2^3/4$ x 4in (7 x 10cm) enlargement you will not be able to judge the performance of a top-quality lens with any degree of accuracy. The quality is clearly revealed only if you choose a bigger enlargement. In practice, at least 10 x 8in (18 x 24cm) is used for this purpose.

You can "feel" whether a knife is sharp.

The sharpness of a photograph is assessed by the human eye. A picture appears sharp, i. e. to have sufficient detail, if we are unable to perceive any loss of detail. The impression of sharpness is very relative, and we must investigate the functions of the human eye more closely if we wish to advance to the limits of the conception of "sharpness".

The light-sensitive layer proper is the retina at the back of the eyeball. It consists of rods and cones. The cones are designed for daylight vision, and arranged in the centre in a pattern resembling that of a honeycomb. To distinguish between two separate details it is necessary that between two stimulated cones one remains unstimulated. Normally we are able to differentiate an angle of 1 min of arc. Resolving power exceeds this only in special cases, e. g. when we see a wire against a clear sky, because here the stimulus affects only a single row of cones, or in the case of the so-called "vernier sharpness", where lines gradually approach each other with decreasing displacement until they are continuous.

In the close-up range, with which we are mostly concerned when we look at photographs, the resolving power at a viewing distance of 10in (25cm) is $1/10$mm; under vernier conditions, however, it is possible to differentiate as little as $4/100$mm. If you apply these standards to your photographs you will find a picture pin sharp if at 5 x magnification it shows unsharpness of not more than $1/10$mm. The 5 x magnification is necessary, since your standard focal length is 50mm, for the following reason: The perspective effect corresponds to reality if the viewing distance in cm has the same numerical value as the focal length of the camera lens x magnification factor.

The term resolving power is used also in connection with the photographic lens and emulsion. Here, too, it is a measure of the degree of detail still reproduced distinctly. The Leicaflex lenses reach their highest resolving power already between f/2.8 and f/4. But because the position of the film is not always sufficiently plane for the best performance of the lens to be utilized without tolerance, and in practice you have to stop down very often if only to gain depth of field, it is also interesting to know at what stage the performance of the lens deteriorates owing to the lens aperture being reduced. The decisive factor here is the diffraction of the light, which becomes increasingly noticeable as the lens is stopped down. Here is a rule of thumb which may serve as a rough guide (without consideration of the other properties of the lens):

Aperture stop in μ = resolving power in lines/mm.

Here is an example: At f/8 = 8 μ = $^1/_{125}$mm, at f/4 = 4 μ = $^1/_{250}$mm resolving power 125 and 250 lines/mm respectively. We have now determined the resolving power of the lens.

The effective performance will be obtained only in connection with the exposure material used. The resolving power of the film is influenced by the silver bromide structure of the photographic emulsion, its thickness and its reaction to halation. Since the emulsion is a turbid medium, which strongly diffuses the light entering it, optimum resolving power can be expected only after correct exposure.

As a rule resolving power is no longer measured in lines/mm today; but the term "contrast transfer function" now used in place of the old expression is very difficult to explain to the layman.

You cannot test the performance of a lens by photographing a newspaper at a distance of 1m (40in). The distance should be more than 20m (66ft), and objects most suitable are a large brick building or other structures with regular patterns. It is sometimes useful to rotate the camera through 45° around its optical axis so that the format diagonal can be evaluated for the picture, e. g. of a row of houses.

120

THE PROPERTIES OF FILMS

The demands we expect a film to meet differ according to the task for which we intend to use it. No one film combines all the desirable properties. If we require maximum speed, graininess is more obtrusive, we shall therefore use such films only if photography with finegrain films is not possible because of insufficient light.

Generally we use films of medium speed (40–200 ASA), in which the various properties add up to the most favourable general performance. Several characteristics must be assessed in a film. These are discussed at length on the following pages to enable you to make a suitable choice.

The manufacture of photographic material requires much expertise and attention to detail. The properties can be altered by bad storage conditions. Humidity and heat have an adverse effect. If stored in a cool and dry place, black-and-white films will keep considerably beyond the expiry date stamped on their containers.

Use well-tried material, i.e. films with whose properties you are familiar, for important subjects. The same speed rating given by different manufacturers does not indicate that the other properties of the films are also the same. The development of the films, too, plays an important part in the uniformity of the results.

1. General sensitivity

The exposure time to be given a film depends on the general sensitivity of the emulsion. In Germany, this is measured in DIN degrees. An increase of 3 DIN represents a doubling of the film speed; thus a 20 DIN film is twice as fast as a 17 DIN one. In Anglo-Saxon countries film speed is measured in ASA; here the progression is arithmetical, i.e. double the ASA value represents double the speed (80 ASA = 2 x speed of 40 ASA).

The exposure meter of the Leicaflex is balanced so that it gives correct values for colour reversal films. Depending on your method of development you can use shorter exposure times for black-and-white films. You can often expose your film at twice the rated speed with impunity (exception: snow scenes). An even higher film speed utilization should be attempted only after careful tests. Please note that the latest change in the DIN rating, although it means an increase of 3 in the numerical value, does not mean an increase in the film speed itself. Example: the previous rating of 19° DIN now corresponds to 22 DIN. The reason for this change is that the somewhat excessive speed reserves had to be reduced and exposure times no longer than necessary for a well balanced negative ensured.

2. Gradation

Our subjects have tone values very delicately graded according to light and colour. The total range of these tone values may extend from the most brilliant whites to the deepest blacks, or show only very minor differences in brightness, according as you photograph a contre-jour motif in glowing sunlight or a subject in a dull autumn mist.

Within certain limits, a film of normal gradation will reproduce the various brightness values of your camera subject at the same gradation as the eye sees them. A soft gradation cuts down the difference between the various tone values and is therefore able to reproduce greater lighting contrasts. Slight brightness differences, on the other hand, are intensified by a film of hard gradation. It introduces brilliance into subjects of poor contrast. What it cannot do is render great differences in brightness at their correct tone values.

Gradation depends mainly on the type of the film; it can, however, also be altered considerably by the method and duration of development. Compensating development is a method used to obtain a suitable gradation in normal to contrasty films for the accommodation of strong lighting contrasts.

Density is reproduced graphically according to an agreed system to make possible a correct classification of films of different gradation. The curve obtained with this method indicates the "characteristics" of a film. This method is used to evaluate also the properties of developers. The contrast of a film is the stronger the steeper the curve. The tangent of the angle formed by the straight-line portion of the film and the abscissa represents the "gamma value". Such measurements can be carried out only by means of densitometric instruments to which the average photographer has no access; he can therefore not check the gamma value. It is, however, very useful in practice to photograph a step wedge, which can be obtained from the film manufacturers' technical information departments. Such a step wedge, or grey scale, constitutes a "standard object", which enables you, when you compare it with the gradation in the negative, quickly to determine whether an emulsion is "soft," "normal", or "contrasty".

3. Colour sensitivity

Originally, the silver bromide crystals in the photographic emulsion are not sensitive to light of all colours. Their range of colour sensitivity is expanded only by the admixture of suitable dyes (sensitization) during emulsion making. Films that have not been sensitized register only ultra-violet and blue. If a film is sensitive to green and yellow it is called "orthochromatic". Films sensitive to all colours including red are described as "panchromatic". In 35mm photography, normally only panchromatic films are used. The designations "panchromatic", "rectepanchromatic" and "orthopanchromatic" are synonymous. If non-sensitized films are required for special tasks, ordinary positive film should be used (obtainable in bulk only, develop in Rodinal 1:50 for 5 minutes at 20° C). Exposure tests should be made as the general sensitivity of the films is low. The only orthochromatic films still available in the Leica format are document-copying films.

All these films are black and white, translating colour values into grey steps of various brightness. It is difficult for the beginner to visualize this translation, above all because this takes place not according to our visual impression but with considerable deviations. Even when an emulsion is sensitized, the translation into grey tones will be inaccurate. In daylight the film is excessively sensitive to blue and ultra-violet. If you want to photograph, for instance, a beautiful blue sky with white clouds, you must first eliminate this hyper-sensitivity to blue. You can do this by means of filters. Depending on the colour and density of such filters you can lighten or darken certain colours and render them accordingly in grey values.

"White light" is not colourless, but constitutes the sum of the entire spectrum. You can easily verify this by inserting a prism in a parallel light beam and splitting up the light into its spectral colours (shown diagrammatically in the illustration). The adjacent, no longer visible wave ranges directly affect photographic emulsions (ultra-violet) or can be made effective through special sensitizing agents (infra-red). The following points must be observed in photographic technique: colours reflected by an object are practically never pure spectral colours; other colours, too, are reflected to a greater or lesser extent. Even on panchromatic films the effect may differ considerably from our visual impression. This is why it is so difficult to assess this translation into grey values correctly in advance. In this respect colour is simpler than black-and-white photography.

4. Grain and graininess

"Grain" is the term for the semolina-like structure which often has a disturbing effect in big enlargements. What we really see is "graininess", i. e. a conglomeration of silver crystals that have coalesced during the developing process.

"Graininess" refers to the developed emulsion, whereas "grain" is used to describe the undeveloped silver halide crystals, which are so small that they become clearly visible only in the microscope at a magnification of 1000 x.

The thickness of the emulsion influences the grain structure because it decisively affects the distribution of the silver bromide crystals. Slow, thinly coated films display the least graininess after development.

During enlarging, light passes through the developed emulsion, where it is reflected by the silver grains, diffracted, and partially absorbed; finally it reaches the light-sensitive enlarging paper through the gaps between the grains. Here it produces "graininess".

"Fine-grain developers" are designed to prevent this clumping together into large groups of grains during development. If such a developer calls for a generous exposure, nothing will have been gained. The problem of grain is therefore solved much more easily and reliably by means of the film instead of the developer.

Occasionally, the degree of graininess visible differs in one and the same film. Since the contrast of our photographic subjects varies a great deal, the negatives will accordingly come to be soft or vigorous. In uniformly light grey areas, graininess is more obtrusive on "hard" than on "soft" bromide paper.

If you want to use graininess deliberately as an effect for pictorial purposes, expose ultra-high-speed film somewhat generously, and develop it for 7—8 minutes in Rodinal 1:50.

Left: Flooded street at Ybbs/Danube. The intensity of the street lamps at night is so high that they are always reproduced with considerable halation. The brightness range is sometimes as large as 1 : 100,000. Even the eye sees a halo at such high contrasts.

Within the last few years the antihalation protection of the films has been vastly improved; nevertheless, a certain amount of halation cannot be avoided.

Right: Lurgrotte cave near Semmriach/Styria. Here, too, light sources are pictured in the background of the scene, but the impressions they give are completely different since the light is scattered not in the film, but by air saturated with water vapour. The dark edges in the left foreground in front of the backlit expanse have nowhere been eroded. Because the light sources are invisible in the picture, the lighting contrast is considerably less than in the picture on the right.

5. Freedom from halation

Haloes are produced by strong lighting contrasts during the exposure. Around the light source appearing in the picture a halo, a "flare", is formed. We distinguish between a diffusion and a reflection halo; the former is caused by diffusion within the emulsion layer, the latter by reflection from the emulsion base. Both forms usually occur in combination.

125

In thin-film emulsions the diffusion halo is reduced. Measures against the reflection halo during film manufacture include dyed backings or intermediate layers, or dyeing of the emulsion base.

6. Resolving power and contour sharpness

Resolving power is the ability to distinguish finest details at a certain distance. In addition to the graininess of the photographic emulsion, the following factors influence resolving power: 1. the contrast of the camera subject, 2. the diffusion halo, 3. the gradation of the film, 4. the wave length of the light, and 5. the quality of the lens in the camera. For the determination of resolving power, lines, screens, radial grids, and similar patterns are used.

This test requires critical focusing and exact exposure and development. Although graininess and resolving power are closely related, they are different phenomena. The resolving power of a thin-film emulsion may be higher than that of a finer-grain, but considerably thicker emulsion. It is adversely affected by overexposure. Development, too, is not without influence. Especially surface developers such as Rodinal or Perinal, which do not attack the emulsion in depth, produce good resolving power, although they do not act as finegrain developers.

Contour sharpness is a term that has come to be used in photography only recently. It is an objective measure of the acutance (sharpness performance) of a film, which is independent of graininess and gradation; but diffusion halation has a decisive influence on it. Contour sharpness is determined through a slit of $^{15}/_{1000}$mm width. Exposure is by contact printing without the use of a lens.

What film to choose?

Films are classified in groups according to their speed. If a film is unknown to you, study the data given by the manufacturer. Check the readings of your own exposure meter with comparable figures of these data. If you find considerable differences, you must be very careful, and are well advised to record the data and to correct them after development.

I first photographed the farm-house in the glancing morning sun. When I came closer I discovered this little kitten in a window. 50mm Summicron f/8, $^1/_{125}sec$.

1. Ultra-high-speed films (above 200 ASA, 24 DIN)

Special films for poor lighting conditions. Latest types up to 800 ASA, 30 DIN. Main uses: in the home without flash, indoor reportages, theatre, circus, variety shows, street scenes at night, bad weather, rain, blizzards.

Gradation: now normal to contrasty. Development: finegrain developers are recommended. If possible, time development in complete darkness.

Exposure: good results only with accurate exposure (short rather than generous). Overexposure increases graininess, and reduces resolving power. If possible utilize the entire format.

2. Normal or medium-speed films (40–200 ASA, 17–24 DIN)

The most versatile films, of the most favourable properties. Their speed is almost invariably adequate for ordinary daylight, and their resolving power higher than that of ultra-high-speed film. The low graininess permits part-enlargements to be made. These films have a wider exposure latitude. It must be borne in mind that in spite of the same speed rating, different brands may have different characteristics, which become evident mainly through different developing times.

3. Slow-speed films (12–32 ASA, 12–16 DIN)

Special films for extreme enlargements. Their very thin emulsion and high resolving power reproduce the finest detail without any disturbing grain structure. Thin-film emulsions demand accurate exposure. To become familiar with such films you should take a series of graduated exposures when in doubt. Exposures are longer because of the slow speed, and the danger of camera shake is accordingly increased. It is better to open up the diaphragm than to choose too slow a shutter speed.

4. Black-and-white reversal film, 35mm panchromatic

Special films for the direct production of transparencies. The reversal process produces a transparency ready for projection directly from the film in the camera. This method is unsurpassed in tone scale, freedom from halation, and fine grain. But the film demands accurate exposure for, as in the colour reversal film, its exposure latitude is very strictly limited. This material affords excellent training in accurate exposure, and the experience gained here is applicable especially when you use colour reversal film. This type of film is most convenient for book copying, since it produces a first-class transparency, superior in cleanness to a printed transparency, at minimum effort. You can obtain a negative should you ever need one without difficulty by contact printing on positive film, or, if top quality is essential, by enlarging the original on sheet film; an increase in contrast can be avoided by generous exposure and short development. As with colour reversal films standard reversal processing is included in the retail price of these films; they are available from Agfa–Gevaert, Kodak (USA) and ORWO. If you are familiar with darkroom routine you can carry out reversal processing yourself.

5. Document copying films

Films of extremely fine grain, very high resolving power, and contrasty gradation. Two types are available; they differ in their colour sensitivity (orthochromatic-panchromatic). Often supplied in bulk only, Agfa Agepe and Agfa Agepan film can now also be bought in 36-exposure daylight cartridges. No speed is indicated on the container. The starting figure for exposure measurement lies between 4 and 16 ASA, 7–13 DIN; the higher speed is obtained with contrasty development, which, however, narrows the exposure latitude very much.

Development is always individual and must be adapted to the purpose of the exposures. This calls for a certain amount of experience. Readily adjustable developers such as Rodinal 1:50 to 1:100 produce excellent results. Developing times vary between 5 and 10 minutes.

Applications: line reproductions, landscapes of low contrast, product photography, photomicrography.

6. Infra-red films

Several brands are on the market in the Leica format. Since these films are also sensitive to ordinary light, this must be suppressed by an infra-red filter. Depending on the make, the sensitivity ranges up to 8500nm. The keeping quality is low at high infra-red sensitivity; the film should be kept in a cool place. Further information on exposure technique will be found on p. 136.

Commercial varieties of 35mm film

Only standard film cartridges, but no Leica metal cassettes, can be used in the Leicaflex. The range of 35mm cartridges on the market is very varied; they contain films of 20 or 36-exposure lengths, and should be used only once.

The film consists of the emulsion base, which today is almost invariably safety base, i. e. not readily inflammable. The thickness of the base ranges between 0.1 and 0.13mm. A grey-blue dye reduces reflection halation; it does not disappear during processing, and prolongs exposure slightly during the positive process. Anti-halation measures have recently been improved. A coloured layer is applied either to the back of the emulsion base or as an intermediate film; it is dissolved by either the developer or the fixing solution. The keeping qualities of photographic emulsions are not unlimited. The properties of the material and the method of storage are of particular importance here. Exposure to humidity is bad, especially at high temperatures. Special film containers are therefore used for the tropics. Repeated change in the storage conditions also reduces the keeping qualities. It is best to keep films in a cool and dry place. Favourable conditions improve keeping qualities so that the date stamped on the container can be exceeded. Nevertheless check the condition of the emulsion by means of trial exposures. Often the general sensitivity is reduced, which you can allow for when you know about it. In the standard 35mm cartridge the film is wound on to a spool, emulsion side inwards. The outer shell is made of plastic or metal. Since the cartridge mouth is not absolutely light tight, the cartridges, whether they contain unexposed or exposed film, should not be left lying in the open for prolonged periods. After the last exposure the film is wound back into the cartridge so that it can be removed from the camera in daylight. For development the cartridge is opened in the darkroom and the film cut off the cartridge spool.

FILTERS AND THEIR USES

Originally the photographic emulsions were almost colour-blind, because their sensitivity was limited to ultra-violet and blue. Such "unsensitized" emulsions are still available today for special purposes. They reproduce blue almost as white, red almost as black, i. e. as the exact opposites to what our visual perception conveys. There is no need for the use of filters here, as such emulsions serve for the reproduction of black-and-white originals only.

Emulsions become sensitive to colours other than blue with the addition of certain dyes during manufacture. Films are called "orthochromatic" if they are sensitive to all colours except red and panchromatic if they are sensitive also to red.

The term of colour sensitivity extends also to black-and-white photography although it is only the grey tones, not the real colours, that are reproduced here. Colour contrasts as marked as between green and red or yellow and blue will in certain conditions produce almost the same grey tone. A better gradation is obtained with the use of a suitable filter. In the past there was much talk about correct tone rendering. But since any translation of a colour into a grey value means an abstraction stronger filters should in certain conditions be chosen if this ensures improved reproduction. To be able to choose a suitable filter, you must consider its effect on the emulsion, not on your eye. For colour films, U. V. absorbing and polarizing filters can be used; yellow, yellow-green, and orange filters are suitable for black-and-white films only.

The use of filters on the Leicaflex SL

Since the exposure meter is installed behind the lens, the filter factor ought to be automatically allowed for in the measurement when a filter is used. But this is not so, because the photo-resistor is more sensitive to the long-wave region of the spectrum than the film. Exposure should be increased beyond the measured value by half a lens stop for a yellow filter and by a full lens stop for yellow-green and orange filters. When you use a polarizing filter, measure the exposure without the filter and treble it.

131

Table of filter factors

(for Leicaflex SL see chapter "Exposure Measurement" p. 62)

Filter	Daylight	Artificial Light
U. V. absorbing	0	0
Yellow	2	1.5
Yellow-green	3	1.5
Orange	3	2.5
Polarizing	3	3

U.V. absorbing filter (colourless)

Photographic emulsions are sensitive not only to visible light, they record also the invisible ultra-violet radiation. The U.V.-a filter, as its name implies, suppresses ultra-violet radiation. The effect of U.V. radiation in ordinary photography is not very great, since modern lenses transmit only small amounts of U.V. radiation.

Only at altitudes of more than 2,500m (8,500ft) will the U.V. content of the light increase appreciably under a cloudless sky and in the absence of haze. Your skin, too, will notice the difference.

The U.V. absorbing filter is practically colourless and therefore particularly well suited for colour film. On the beach, for instance, it is a most effective safeguard against salt crystals and sand. The filter factor is so small that it can be ignored. If you wish you may leave your U.V. filter permanently on your lens, except for street scenes in the evening with neon light advertising and light sources in the picture area.

Yellow filter

The yellow filter is the universal filter for landscape photography where only the blue sky has to be "adjusted". It ensures approximately correct tone rendering without too much contrast in the sky. Snow pictures are generally attractive only in sunlight. Because the shadows are blue a yellow filter is indispensable unless you want to use the even more contrasty orange filter.

The summit of the extinct volcano Ercyes Dag, 13,120ft (4000m) in Central Anatolia. 50mm Summicron-R. Top: through yellow filter, bottom: through orange filter.
Photograph by Hans Gsellmann.

Yellow-green filter

The effect of the yellow-green filter closely resembles that of the yellow filter. It should be used like the latter; in landscapes, it reproduces green tones a little lighter; suntanned skin is not quite as light as through the yellow filter. The exposure factor is slightly higher (table p. 132).

Orange filter

The orange filter already belongs to the class of the contrast filters. You can exaggerate a blue summer sky with white clouds. It renders blue and green tones darker. In snow pictures the shadows will be darker than in reality. Long-distance subjects are often improved because the long-wave rays transmitted by the orange filter penetrate haze more effectively.

Polarizing filter

The various effects of the polarizing filter are still too little known. It can be used far more widely than you would assume. Especially in colour photography you will find it worth while to study its effect: look at the subject through the filter while rotating the filter through 180°.

The polarizing filter proper is cemented between two sheets of plane glass. Its effect is due to the fact that polarized light vibrates in one plane only, whereas ordinary light vibrates in all directions. A large proportion of ordinary light striking reflecting, non-metallic surfaces will be reflected after becoming polarized. Since a polarizing filter transmits only light vibrating in a single plane the reflected light can be extinguished if the polarizing filter is used in a position where it is crossed with the vibration direction of the reflected light. The degree of polarization depends on the angle of reflection, extinction is therefore not always complete. It is easy to use this filter. After removing the retaining ring, screw the polarizing filter into the filter thread of the Leicaflex and, slowly rotating the filter, observe the effect in the viewfinder. The best effect is not always obtained when the reflections are completely removed.

You must remember that when you change between upright and horizontal view the filter effect is strongly modified by the 90° rotation.

In addition to the well-known effect of eliminating reflections during the photography of furniture, glassware and water surfaces, the influence of the polarizing filter on colour subjects is particularly interesting. It is favourable in many landscape subjects with green expanses, because by extinguishing the reflections of the blue sky it intensifies the green tones. The blue of the sky itself, too, becomes darker in certain directions. Since polarizing filters absorb ultra-violet, they also increase the contrast in long-distance subjects.

A new version of the polarizing filter in simple Series VII mount when used on the Leicaflex SL offers the advantage of the exposure factor being included in the measurement. It is a circularly polarizing filter, to be placed in the new lens hood and rotated with the knurled knob (see p. 78) until the best effect is obtained; this can be clearly seen in the viewfinder.

At a certain angle, window panes reflect so strongly that one cannot see through them any more. It is a well-known fact that polarizing filters eliminate such reflections, because these consist of polarized light. Similar effects can be obtained on sheets of water. Since polarizing filters are practically grey, they can also be used with colour films. The filter factor is about 3x. In special conditions, when a large quantity of polarized light is being extinguished, it will be higher.

Both photographs: 90 mm Elmarit-R. Top: f/8, ¹/₆₀sec, bottom: f/8, ¹/₂₀sec, with polarizing filter.

Photograph by Günter Osterloh

Infra-red photography

The wave range of the light adjacent to the visible red is called "infra-red". It is invisible to the eye, but can be utilized for photography with films which are specially sensitized for it.

Infra-red rays penetrate atmospheric haze much more effectively than ordinary light. The green of foliage, which contains chlorophyll, also reflects infra-red rays. This produces unusual effects. The far distance becomes clearer and more contrasty, the blue of the sky or a sheet of water black, whereas green meadows and the leaves of the trees appear as white as snow.

Infra-red films are sensitive not only to infra-red, but also to ordinary light. In order to eliminate this portion of the rays, a dark red filter is used. Since the camera lenses are not computed for the long-wave infra-red rays the distance setting must be corrected; the camera extension must be increased by about $1/300$ of the focal length of the lens, and the following distances should be set instead of ∞:

	focal length	
50mm	15m (50ft)	
90mm	27m (90ft)	at f/11 or f/16
135mm	40m (132ft)	

In spite of its interesting effect, infra-red photography is of only minor importance, mainly because sharpness is not at its best here. The long-wave rays have an inherently reduced resolving power, and the camera lenses are not well enough corrected for this region of the spectrum.

View from the summit of the Valuga, Arlberg, Austria. Typical change of the pictorial appearance by means of infra-red light.

Top: Normal exposure on a sunlit, slightly hazy day. Bottom: Exposure through an infra-red filter. All portions containing chlorophyll (foliage of the trees, meadows) strongly reflect infra-red light, and therefore appear light in the positive. The distance haze is penetrated; this results in a completely altered transition to the background. This effect is of value for scientific purposes, but should be used with restraint by the amateur.

Both photographs with 90mm Elmarit-R. Top: f/11, 1/250sec, without filter, 40 ASA/ 17 DIN film. Bottom: f/11, 1/4sec, Kodak infra-red film; infra-red filter.

FLASH PHOTOGRAPHY

The coach from Toronto stops, disgorging its load of tourists: "Here you see Niagara Falls" the guide is trying to make himself heard above the roar of the water, "3000ft wide, 200ft high, and more than a mile away" — and the first flash pierces the darkness of the night across the thundering masses of water in their ghostlike flood-lighting. A tiny reflector, and a huge distance! What is the use of a flashbulb here? A time exposure from a tripod on high-speed film and at full aperture is more likely to be successful. Our flash can achieve much, and at short distances may have a stronger effect than the sun. But the quantity of its light is limited, and its effect decreases as the object distance increases.

Nevertheless, flash photography has become more and more popular during recent years, and the equipment for it lighter and handier. We distinguish between two types of flash unit, of basically different design.

1. Electronic flash units

The unit consists of a tube filled with an inert gas, an ignition coil, and a capacitor, which permits the storage of electrical energy.

The capacitor is charged by means of a battery and, controlled by the camera contact, transmits its accumulated energy to the flash tube within about $1/1000$ sec. Since the inert gas does not burn, but only lights up, the tube can be used again and again.

The performance of the electronic flash units varies widely; the light-weight and moderately-priced amateur units have only limited power. If you take flash photographs frequently you will find the use of electronic flash more economical. Such a flash unit, however, demands careful maintenance, for its performance depends on the state of the battery and of the electrolytic con-

For interior work in moderately-sized rooms it is urgently recommended not to attach the flash lamp to the Leicaflex. A better-balanced illumination is obtained if the flash lights the scene indirectly via the ceiling. There is a loss of light intensity, i.e. the lens should be opened by 1–2 stops, but disturbing shadows in the background are avoided.

Top: Flash lamp mounted directly on the camera, f/11, $1/60$sec.

Bottom: Flash illuminates the group via the ceiling (bounce flash). f/5.6, $1/60$sec.

denser, which loses its electric formation unless it is used at certain intervals. Mains-operated flash units should be charged for 10—15 minutes before the flash is fired if they had not been used for some time. The manufacturers' instructions should be strictly observed, as they vary widely between different brands. The following simple test whether the contact of the Leicaflex functions correctly is recommended: connect all the parts according to the instructions, open the camera back and place a piece of bromide paper on the film guide (this can be done in subdued light). Remove the camera lens and hold the flashlamp directly in front of the aperture — release. The effect of the flash will be visible on the photographic paper directly, even without development.

2. Flashbulbs

Flashbulbs contain combustible metal and oxygen. They can therefore be used only once, since after firing they are completely burnt out. The time lapse between ignition and the peak brightness of the combustion (in the mean about $1/60$ sec) depends on the size and make of the flashbulbs. In the Leicaflex the contact for flashbulbs is adjusted to certain types of lamp and their firing delay.

Expendable-flash units as they are called are very small and light and require little maintenace. The brightness of the various flashbulbs is reliably constant. The bulbs vary greatly in size, and the power of the largest types is far superior to that of electronic flash. Blue-tinted flashbulbs are necessary for colour photography.

The latest development has produced flash cubes, combining four flashbulbs in a unit. After the first flash has been fired the cube is turned through 90°, when the second flash will be ready for use. The third and fourth flashes are operated accordingly. The main advantages of the flash cube are its rapid exposure sequence and its space-saving volume. Table of flashbulbs see p. 26.

Automatic production control by means of closed-circuit television at the Daimler-Benz works, Stuttgart. 21mm Super-Angulon-R, 125 ASA (22 DIN) film. Top: f/11, $1/30$sec, direct flash. Bottom: f/8, $1/15$sec, bounce flash.   Photographs by Rudolf Seck

Guide number

The guide number has been introduced as a practical measure for flash photography. Its use calls for a simple calculation:

$$\frac{\text{Guide number}}{\text{Flash distance}} = \text{lens stop}$$

$$\frac{\text{Guide number}}{\text{Lens stop}} = \text{flash distance}$$

The guide number is based on the following principles: the reflected light quantity is inversely proportional to the square of the flash/object distance, and the speed of the lens to the square of the aperture stop number. Since both values change as their squares, they can be used alternatively. But the actual guide number deviates from the ideal value, because light reflected by the surroundings must be allowed for.

The guide number therefore represents only an average value for subjects in average rooms at medium distances and where the light is reflected by the walls and ceiling. In small and bright rooms the guide number increases because of the good reflection; large rooms with dark walls and outdoor subjects reduce it. This applies also to subjects within the close-up range, where there is no reflected light. Guide numbers are therefore variable and depend on

1. the ASA (DIN) rating of the film

2. the reflecting power of the room and the subject

3. the developing process (only little effect).

A guide number for 50 ASA (18 DIN) is adapted to higher and lower film speeds according to the following scheme:

ASA	12	25	50	100	200	400	800
DIN	12	15	18	21	24	27	30
Factor	0.5	0.7	1	1.4	2	2.8	4

Since the processing of colour film is strictly standardized, the guide number is today generally based on colour film. If a special value is given for colour film, it can be used for black-and-white film of the same speed without risk

THE WAY TO MANUAL SKILL

Every instrument demands a certain dexterity for its operation; the Leicaflex is no exception. If you want to obtain top-class results, it is not enough for you to take photographs "in earnest" only when you are faced with a worthwhile subject; a certain amount of training beforehand, "playing about with the camera", is recommended. A pianist about to play in a concert, too, is already skilled at playing his instrument; nevertheless he practises the whole work or difficult passages of it beforehand. It is true that there are many occasions in photography when time is no object, on the other hand, we have all come to realize that only complete mastery of the camera leads to success. The following suggestions have been well tried in many courses of photography. Whether you are a beginner, advanced, or already an old hand, there are many exercises, culminating in true virtuosity when you can shoot from above with outstretched arms, from the hip from below, without looking through the viewfinder.

Until you are really familiar with your Leicaflex, practise — at first without film — holding it for upright and horizontal pictures, working the smooth shutter release, focusing according to the operating instructions. As you become familiar with the exposure meter, practise changing lens aperture and shutter speed. Since your subconscious plays a decisive role in the smooth handling of your camera it is not enough to understand how these functions interact, you must repeat all manipulations until they become automatic. This "automation", however, often demands that you strictly adhere to the correct sequence. This is particularly important with film loading and unloading. Every mistake results in a loss of many exposures. The likelihood of making mistakes is greatest with exciting, unrepeatable shots.

Practising without a film is a preliminary stage, it is simple and cheap, but results cannot be checked. As you learn how to swim only in the water, you will learn how to take photographs only when you practise on real film. In order to keep costs within reasonable limits, you may use out-of-date film You may also want to develop the film without making positives; you can evaluate it by means of a 5 x magnifier or of projecting the negative in a 35mm projector.

Before you open the camera back, always make sure that there is no film that has not been rewound left in the camera, i. e. swing out and turn the rewind crank; if you feel any resistance, rewind before opening the back.

Insert the film as described on p. 42; satisfy yourself that the rewind crank turns against the arrow when you make the two blank exposures necessary to transport unexposed film into the film window for the first exposure. This is an important check.

Camera tilt and camera shake occur more frequently with upright than with horizontal pictures. Your first step should therefore be to practise photographing doors and windows in the upright view. Verticals must not converge, at the same time the format should be well utilized. To make this possible, the camera lens should be directed approximately at the point of intersection of the diagonals of the picture area. In order to check focusing and camera shake, take photographs of large posters. For the next exposure, too, stick to stationary objects, so that you can still operate all the controls of the camera at leisure. Examine the background as well as the surrounding field; look for objects where you can focus on the foreground and use a large aperture with high shutter speed. Now take the same picture, focusing on the background at full aperture, and as a third variant focusing on the front third, stopping down to f/11 or f/16 and adjusting the shutter speed accordingly.

36 exposures offer a large scope for variations; don't take your subjects too seriously, all they are required to do is improve your manual skill with your new camera. Your first trial film should not be your last. Expose one film per week; when you start your holiday after four weeks you will be surprised at the amount of exposure technique you have learned during your short period of training.

The second stage deals with movement studies. For the sharp reproduction of a given subject certain minimum shutter speeds are required: for a pedestrian approaching you $1/125$ sec is enough; if he moves at right angles to the camera, use $1/250$ sec. Walking persons are excellent for these experiments. The characteristic picture of a pedestrian should be a side view; it is more typical, because the step conveys the movement better. The best moment is when the foot, after advancing, touches the ground. You can most effectively capture this moment if you count "left, right, left, right" as your subject approaches your picture area, on which you should already have focused; you will not have time for this when the movement is actually in progress.

Photograph by Prof. Franz Hoppichler

What distance do you choose in order to utilize your film format adequately? Start with the horizontal view, because this is easier. Take the medium height of a person as about 5ft 10in. Deviations range between 5ft 4in and 6ft 4 in, i. e. less than 10% of the average height. Your picture needs a little space at the top and bottom — imagine a frame 8ft high, 12ft wide. Let your groups walk through this frame. With the 50mm lens a distance of 17ft (5m) is correct, with the 90mm lens 30ft (9m), and with the 135mm lens 44ft (13.5m). At the same time, the much simplified formula, which you can use when your subject is 100 x the focal length of your lens or further away, is worth remembering:

$$100 \times 50 \text{ mm} = 17\text{ft (5m)}$$
$$100 \times 24\text{mm} = 8\text{ft (2.4 m)}$$
$$100 \times 36\text{mm} = 11\text{ft (3.6m)}$$

Naturally, you need some extra space for a walking group. For the 50mm lens the permissible tolerance lies between 15ft (4.5m) and 18ft (5.5m). Mark both distances, and you are ready for practising. The depth of field is sufficient even if you expose $^1/_{125}$ sec at f/2.8.

You will find that 17ft (5m) is much too short a distance for sports, i. e. very rapidly moving, subjects. If you want to take a frontal view you will be in the way, and lateral views are often impossible because of the fencing or cordons. The obvious conclusion that with a 90mm or 135mm lens you will obtain results that fill your format better than from a more convenient distance is confirmed in practice. It is also recommended as a good exercise to follow up 50mm shots of walking persons immediately with variants through the 90mm or 135mm lens. The longer focal length offers the following advantages here: the three-dimensionality is enhanced, because the pictorially important element emphasized by critical focus stands out most clearly against the blurred background. Owing to the narrower angle of view the background becomes more restful, as its area is more restricted. Furthermore, the size of your moving subject changes less rapidly in the viewfinder, because on account of its longer distance its reproduction ratio, too, changes less rapidly. You will, however, find that detailed knowledge of these conditions through persistent practice is essential. Choose a fast rather than a slow shutter speed, because the danger of camera shake increases with the focal length of your camera lens.

Photographs by H. Gsellmann

In the preceding paragraph the technique of correct shutter release at a certain movement phase has been described. The next stage will teach you to apply the sureness of touch you have acquired so that you can pay proper attention to the aspect of pictorial composition. This means that you should choose your point of view so as to capture the suitable phase of movement from the correct angle of view, in the most favourable light, against a suitable background. At this "advanced level" experts liberally modify a number of standards. A high degree of skill is needed to photograph a moving subject with a slow enough shutter speed to make the movement blur a pictorial asset. It means making a virtue out of necessity. Unfortunately, convincing success is rare in this sphere, for only very few photographers have managed to find, by trial and error, the correct amount of unsharpness to ensure the best effect. Success is far more assured of pictures of fast-moving subjects such as races if you work with an average shutter speed, e.g. $1/250$ sec, and follow your subject with your camera during the exposure. The main

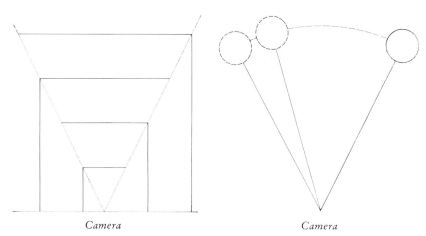

Camera   Camera

Left: The dotted lines indicate the angle of field of the 35mm Elmarit-R in the horizontal format. The 90° solid lines intersecting them show clearly that with this focal length camera distance and image width are the same. This knowledge is essential for "blind shooting", taking pictures without looking through the viewfinder.

Right: If you want to take a surprise shot of your subject (circle on the right), for best results focus the camera on equidistant objects (dashed circles), and only "home" on your subject immediately before pressing the button.

feature will then be sharp, but the background will be blurred. You can try this technique on every trunk road by following a passing car with your camera at various shutter speeds. This gives you a feeling for the correct technique; at the next motor racing event you will no longer shoot blindly and have to rely on pot luck for your results.

The technique of taking pictures while you walk — blind shots, etc.

You can take photographs while you walk in the same way as from a moving train or car. But you must not release the shutter any-odd-how: only when your body is resting on one leg, i. e. not when you are about to "put your foot down" — this produces camera shake. If you are looking through the viewfinder, a short pause in the walking movements — as if you were about to let yourself drop to the ground — will be enough for releasing the shutter at a speed of $^1/_{250}$ sec or higher.

If you want to take photographs unnoticed, e. g. in oriental countries, you occasionally have to use the "blind shot" method, an exposure technique in

148

Left: If you are wedged in a crowd of spectators or standing in front of an obstructing fence, hold your Leicaflex high above the obstacle and take a pot-shot at your subject. Especially with the 35 mm Elmarit-R it is not difficult to obtain good results .

Right: The table tripod is so small and light that you can always carry it conveniently in your pocket. Propped against a column or a wall in a church or other indoor locality it permits exposure times of several seconds. With long-focal-length lenses it can also be used as a substitute for a "chestpod".

which you do not look through the viewfinder. Carry your Leicaflex on the neck strap or in the open ever-ready case on your chest, aim with the lens and press the button, looking anywhere but at your camera. Set your shutter speed, distance, and lens aperture beforehand, if necessary with the aid of an object in conditions similar to your subject's. You should have a fair idea of the picture areas to be obtained with the various focal lengths, having previously practised looking through the viewfinder with the different lenses in your camera. This technique is particularly convenient with the 35mm Elmarit-R, because here the object distance equals the width of the picture area.

Another kind of blind shooting involves exposing your film with the camera held with your outstretched arms above the heads of spectators. With 35mm and 50mm lenses, this technique, too, has certain prospects of success. With longer focal lengths you require a lot of practice if you want to be able to evaluate even half the film format in the enlarger.

THE BRIDGE TO THE LEICA SYSTEM

The general wish to be able to use existing Leica lenses on the Leicaflex can be met only within limits, for the following reasons: the flange focal distance for the Leicaflex lenses is 47mm. In the Leicas with screw thread it is 28.8mm, and in the Leica-M models 27.8mm. Furthermore, the diameter of the Leicaflex bayonet is larger. No measuring-viewfinder-coupled Leica lenses can therefore be used directly on the Leicaflex. But since in the ordinary Leica system many lenses can be mounted on the Visoflex I, II, or III, they can also be used on the Leicaflex with an adapter. The adapter ring (14127) has a Leicaflex bayonet on the camera- and a Leica bayonet on the lens side. Its height is 21.8mm, so that the total distance in combination with the Leicaflex is 68.8mm. This is exactly the distance in the Leica with Visoflex II or III. To obtain this value with the Visoflex I a further adapter 16466 must be used (flange focal distance [front thread to film plane] of the Visoflex I: 91.3mm).

The adapter ring has an adjustable simulator cam which transmits the lens aperture values to the exposure meter of the standard Leicaflex. Another version of this adapter, distinguished by an * before the code number, has been designed for the Leicaflex SL: it has a stop for the exposure meter, which permits measurement at the working aperture of the SL. The description in the following paragraphs therefore allows for the difference between the operation of the earlier Leicaflex and that of the Leicaflex SL.

In the Leicaflex the exposure is measured with the Leica lens in exactly the same way as with a Leicaflex lens. The intended lens aperture is reported to

The adapter ring 14127 for using the Leicaflex with the Leica System. The aperture numbers refer to the adjustable simulator cam, which transmits the values to the Leicaflex exposure meter.

*The version *14127 can be used both for the Leicaflex and the Leicaflex SL. A new, less expensive version can be used in the Leicaflex SL. Its Code No. is 14167.*

Leicaflex SL with adapter ring for the 90mm Summicron f/2.

the exposure meter via the simulator cam. The indicated lens aperture must, however, be transferred manually to the Leica lens used. If owing to stopping down or to the increased extension the light intensity sinks below f/5.6 the prisms in the measuring field become darker and the measuring procedure will eventually become very difficult. A combination of the Focusing Bellows II with short-focal-length lenses for macrophotography is therefore not recommended. 90mm and 135mm lenses, on the other hand, are very convenient to use in the Focusing Bellows. If objects smaller than 14 x 21cm (approx. 6 x 8in) are to be photographed exposure factors must be allowed for.

With the Leicaflex SL the *14127 or the 14167 ring adapter must be used. It permits measurement at the working aperture. All exposure factors for the close-up range are also automatically allowed for in the measurement. With small apertures the intensity of the light acting on the exposure meter may become so low that the exposure meter no longer responds. The diaphragm must be opened until a measurement is possible, and the exposure time calculated.

*By means of the adapter ring the Focusing Bellows II can be attached to the Leicaflex.
In macrophotography the 90mm Elmarit and the 135mm Tele-Elmar are preferable
to shorter-focal-length lenses. If the effective light power of a lens sinks below f/5.6,
the microprisms have only limited use for focusing, with consequent limitation of
application in the macro range. This limitation does not apply to the Leicaflex SL,
where the subject is focused on the microscreen of the surrounding field.*

Each step the diaphragm is stopped down requires twice the exposure time
(next lower shutter speed) of the previous stop.

If the central screen becomes too dark, the surrounding field with the microscreen can be used for focusing. Here, too, it may be useful to focus at medium apertures and to set the working aperture only for the actual exposure.

The following table shows the lenses which can be used with the adapter
14127 directly or with the aid of further adapters. If macrophotography only
is required, the short-focal-length Leica lenses, too, can be used, but can be
focused without difficulty in the Leicaflex SL only.

List of Leica lenses suitable for use with the Adapter 14127 **

Focal length	Lens (* lens unit only)	Code-No. or No. of the supp-lementary part	Focusing range	Object size at minimum distance
65 mm	Elmar f/3.5	16 464	∞ – 13'' ∞ – 33 cm	2.3 × 3.3'' 5.8 × 8.7 cm
90 mm	Elmar* f/4 (not all lenses up to ∞)	16 467	∞ – 40'' ∞ 100 cm	8.5 × 12.8'' 21.6 × 32.4 cm
90 mm	Elmarit* f/2.8	16 464	∞ – 20'' ∞ – 50 c m	3.1 × 4.7'' 8 × 12 cm
90 mm	Summicron f/2 (in short mount)	16 462	∞ – 30'' ∞ – 76 cm	5.8 × 8.7'' 14.8 × 22.2 cm
125 mm	Hektor f/2.5	16 466	∞ – 48'' ∞ – 120 cm	7.5 × 11.3'' 19.2 × 28.8 cm
135 mm	Hektor *f/4.5 or Elmar* f/4	⎰16 464 ⎱16 472	∞ – 38'' ∞ – 96 cm	4.7 × 7.1'' 12 × 18 cm
135 mm	Hektor f/4.5 or Elmar f/4 (in short mount)	16 466	∞ – 60'' ∞ – 150 cm	8.5 × 12.7'' 21.6 × 32.4 cm
135 mm	Tele-Elmar* f/4	16 464	∞ – 38'' ∞ – 96 cm	4.7 × 7.1'' 12 × 18 cm
135 mm	Elmarit f/2.8 (in short mount)	16 462	∞ – 62'' ∞ – 155 cm	8.6 × 13'' 22 × 33 cm
200 mm	Telyt f/4 or f/4.5	16 466	∞ – 10' ∞ – 300 cm	12.2 × 18.3'' 31 × 46.5 cm
280 mm	Telyt f/4.8	16 466	∞ – 19' ∞ – 450 cm	17 × 25.5'' 43 × 64.5 cm
400 mm	Telyt f/5	16 466	∞ – 30' ∞ – 750 cm	16 × 24'' 40 × 60 cm
65 mm	Elmar f/3.5	16 556	∞ – 11'' ∞ – 28 cm	6.7 × 10'' 17 × 25.5 mm
90 mm	Elmar* f/4 or Elmarit f/2.8	16 556	∞ – 14'' ∞ – 36 cm	8.6 × 13'' 22 × 33 mm
135 mm	Tele-Elmar* f/4	16 556	∞ – 23'' ∞ – 58 cm	13.8 × 21'' 35 × 53 mm
135 mm	Hektor* f/4.5 or Elmar* f/4	⎰16 556 ⎱16 472	∞ – 22'' ∞ – 56 cm	13.4 × 20'' 34 × 51 mm

** The 14167 adapter is equally suitable.

SMALL ACCESSORIES

Correction lenses

The viewfinder eyepiece of the Leicaflex is mounted so that a correction lens can be clipped on to it. Even without this, spectacle wearers can easily survey the entire viewfinder field. But slight visual defects that do not require the wearing of spectacles can make it impossible to focus accurately enough with the Leicaflex; here a correction lens comes into its own. Your order for this should be accompanied by the prescription for your distance spectacles; details are required only of the eye with which you habitually focus. Only spherical correction lenses are available; astigmatism, which calls for cylindrical lenses, cannot be corrected.

Table tripod and ball-and-socket head

The handy folding table tripod is useful on many occasions. Propped sideways against a wall, a tree, or a pillar in a church it supports the camera even during long exposure times. The ball-and-socket head is a versatile accessory for swivelling and tilting the camera in any desired direction. The top and bottom parts are reversible for $^1/_4$in and $^3/_8$in threads.

Cable release

The cable release with clamping screw should be chosen. This allows you to keep the shutter open as long as required in the "B" setting (long exposure times).

Cases for the Leicaflex

The black ever-ready case of the Leicaflex is cut from a single piece of leather and therefore weatherproof. You can detach the front by pushing the press-stud on the back strongly upwards.

The amateur case has room for a Leicaflex with a lens of 35 to 90mm focal length in position. Another 90 or 135mm lens and a 50 or 35mm lens can be kept in a side compartment; in addition, it accommodates Elpro close-up lenses and filters.

The Universal Case III with Insert III accepts lenses of 35 and 50mm focal length, and two lenses of 90, 135 and 180mm focal length. It also has sufficient space for Elpro close-up lenses in leather cases, filters, and films.

135mm Elmarit-R, f/11, $^1/_{250}$sec, 100 ASA (21 DIN) film. Photograph by Erich Vetter

THE ACTION OF THE LIGHT

Effect of illumination

The most important light source is the sun. With supreme disregard of the photographers' wishes it moves in its daily orbit, hides behind clouds, or blazes from a clear sky. It changes the appearance of an object during the course of the day and the cycle of the seasons.

If you take photography seriously and want to do more than pursue the limited hobby of collecting snapshots, you must develop a kind of "sense of lighting". Close observation, but also your own pictures will soon teach you that the appearance of an object in the morning differs from that at midday, that under a harsh summer sun from that on a dull rainy day.

But even in the uniform lighting conditions of a sunlit day the illumination of a subject changes according to your point of view. There is a close relationship between point of view and illumination. If the sun lights the subject frontally we speak of front lighting. This kind of lighting produces flat pictures, which are usually boring, because they are without enlivening shadows and modelling.

An experiment will show you the effect of different illumination on an object. Look at a section of cobblestones still occasionally found in the old part of a city or town, at first with the sun at your back. Then slowly walk round the cobbles in a semicircle, so that the sun will first shine from one side, and eventually directly in front of you. In frontal lighting the colour of the stones is important; in side- or contre-jour lighting the stones acquire roundness, they almost "come alive".

This experience applies to many objects lit by the sun. Side- and contre-jour light is to be preferred to frontal lighting. You will not always be in a certain place just at the right time, and often you will have no alternative but to wait until the sun is kind enough to make your subject appear in the most favourable light.

If you visit Salzburg, you will want to take a picture of the beautiful panorama from the Café Winkler. Here the difference in lighting between day and night is shown from the same viewpoint. 90mm Elmarit-R, f/8, 1/30sec (top), f/8, 1sec (bottom).

If you are in a hurry passing through the place, you will take the picture all the same if you consider it important enough as a souvenir; but you should be honest enough to admit that you could have done better.

Suitable illumination is of particular importance with architectural subjects. Experts in this field speak of the "critical half hour", by which they mean the short period during which the sunlight moves exactly sideways across the main front of a building. Even a roughcast wall will come to life in this glancing light.

Sunlight out of a clear blue sky is not the photographer's ideal weather. Were he in a position to do so he would order large cumulus clouds for his outdoor work. They act like huge reflectors, whose broadly diffused rays soften the shadows and suffuse everything with a soft light. Hazy sunlight, too, provides a pleasant illumination for foreground subjects. But even if the sun does not shine at all, you need not leave your Leicaflex at home. Subjects without number are most rewarding even in dull weather; rain, as a matter of fact, offers a large variety of unsuspected opportunities. You can photograph hurried passers-by under their umbrellas, reflected in the wet asphalt of the street.

But it is the misty day which provides one of the most fascinating photographic experiences. Mist or fog by blanketing everything is the great simplifier, contrasts are almost suppressed, details disappear, and all that remains is ghostlike shapes merging into the empty grey of the background.

Illumination with artificial light

Whereas in daylight you will only very rarely be able to modify the illumination, and your efforts must be concentrated on the sensible use of the available light, artificial light offers you the prospect of creating your own illumination.

Normally you will start with the main light source and try to illuminate your subject so that its characteristic features stand out clearly. Your next task will be to adjust the light from this first lamp so that the shadows in the final picture are well balanced. You must therefore "retrieve" the light of this

The blurred marginal portions underline the spatial effect. 90mm Elmarit-R, f/4, 1/250sec, 125 ASA/22 DIN film. Photograph by Günter Kisselbach

158

lamp by means of suitable equipment. Portable reflecting screens can be used if the walls of the room are not sufficient for this purpose. The recovery of this light has the big advantage over a second light source in that it allows a much more delicate adjustment.

Only when you have made full use of your main source should you begin to think of a second lamp if necessary. It should be used either for softening the shadows, when it must be considerably weaker than the main light, and the shadows it casts must not be disturbing, or as an effect light, when it may be brighter, but should illuminate only a limited area. The beamed light of a spot (possibly a projector) is very popular as an effect light, because it lights up limited areas intensely from a long distance, making it possible to emphasize certain contours and details.

The lighting of the background, too, plays an important role depending on the shape and colour of your subject. The second lamp is therefore often used for balancing the background brightness so that the subject stands out prominently.

Work with artificial light demands a certain amount of experience. The relative intensity of the various light sources is a very important factor. The optimum degree of contrast depends on the nature of the subject. Since photographic paper reproduces a tone range of only 30:1, differences in intensity of illumination from 1:4 to 1:6 are almost invariably enough. The reflection of the light is measured directly on the subject by means of a sheet of white paper.

Studies in artificial lighting

Top left: How not to do it. The model was sitting on a chair, leaning backwards, thereby producing a double chin. The main light was too frontal. The background was too close, the shadows are therefore obtrusive.

Top right: Strong effect lighting. Three lamps were used; the main light was set up so close and at such a low angle that this stage effect was produced.

The two bottom pictures show clearly the great influence of the main light source. It is reflected by the eyes, and the position of the reflections indicates the direction of the light. Both the cheek and the ear are rendered quite differently. A projection screen was used to soften the contrast.

160

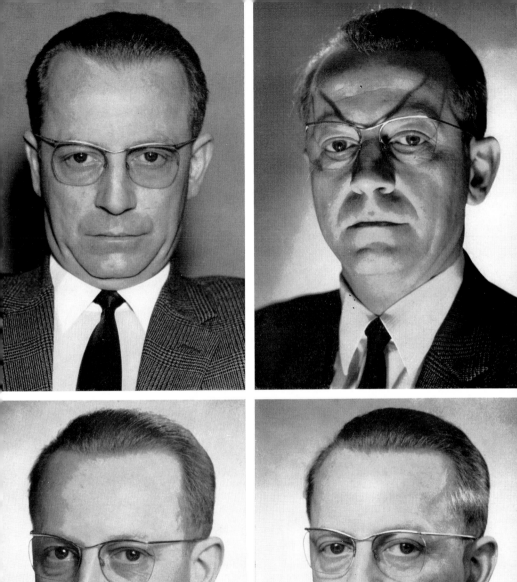

PICTORIAL COMPOSITION

Even the best camera can be no more than a tool. Its achievements depend largely on the "photographic vision" of its user. But you must first learn to appreciate the meaning of "photographic vision", and to distinguish between the vision of the human eye and that of the camera.

1. The eye sees in colour when there is colour. Abstraction into grey tones as with the black-and-white film is not possible.

2. The resolving power of the eye is limited, so that it recognizes details only within a certain distance. Telephoto lenses bridge distances. Infra-red films overcome haze.

3. The angle within which the eye sees really sharp is narrow. The eye adds the visual impressions, and transmits them to the brain, which registers them. The camera "sees" everything between 6° and 92° sharp depending on the lens fitted in it.

4. The eye records a residual image only very briefly ($^1/_{50}$ sec); thereafter, the image disappears. The photographic picture can be fixed.

5. The shortest distance for near vision for the eye is 25cm (minimum distance of comfortable vision). Close-up and macro-photography at multiple magnifications are possible from considerably shorter distances.

6. The eye sees rapid movements only imperfectly. The focal-plane shutter is capable of a speed of $^1/_{2000}$ sec. It records phases of movement in the picture which the eye is hardly able to record.

7. The eye requires a certain level of brightness before it is able to recognize anything at all. A camera needs less light for recording a subject, provided the exposure time is long enough.

The eye senses, the camera lens records. Eye and brain are an organic whole. Memory and emotion have a considerable influence on their function. We do not see objects as they are, but as we are accustomed to see them. By contrast the camera reproduces important and unimportant features with equal emphasis. Since our pair of eyes sees stereoscopically, three-dimensionally, and always through the same pair of lenses, our orientation in space differs from the photographic rendering, where, depending on the focal length of the lens and the camera distance, the perspective changes.

135mm Elmarit-R, f/5.6, $^1/_{250}$sec, 50 ASA/18 DIN film.

Photograph by Prof. St. Kruckenhauser

21mm Super Angulon-R

21mm Super Angulon-R

35mm Elmarit-R

50mm Summicron-R

135mm Elmarit-R

50mm Summicron-R

164

Point of view and picture area are decisive for the reproduction. The various pictures of the Pietà in Wetzlar Cathedral show the great differences in reproduction when not only the viewpoint, but also the focal length is changed. The illumination by ordinary daylight was more or less identical for all exposures.

The art historian must have several aspects of the same object. He will want detailed views to supplement the general aspects. He will use supplementary light sources to bring out whatever detail he finds important.

A sturdy tripod was used for these exposures. The exposure times were the same, f/11, 4sec on Ilford Pan F (50 ASA, 18 DIN). The exposure meter built into the Leicaflex indicated f/5.6 at 1sec. But since it was desirable to use f/11, the exposure time had to be doubled for each next smaller aperture, and extended to 4sec. Had f/16 been used for the exposures, 8sec exposure would have been necessary.

The eye adapts itself to lighting contrasts, it automatically changes its power of distinction when we look at a sunlit landscape from a room. The bridging of such great brightness differences raises difficulties in photography.

In a black-and-white photograph we can translate colours only into grey tones, indicate space only through perspective, show movement only as an instant from a whole sequence. Accordingly light and shade, sharpness and unsharpness are the media appropriate to photography. If you want to become a competent photographer, you must learn to compose your pictures with these elements.

Photographic composition is always based on selection. It is necessary to bring order into, and to simplify, the chaos of impressions received by our eyes. If up to now you have taken little notice of such things, do not say "I have no talent"; "I have no experience" is more apt. We live in an age that continuously feeds us with pictures in illustrated papers, journals, the cinema and on television. All you have to do for your photographic achievements to improve is look more closely at the formal principles of composition. Here, too, then, trial films are a great help. Your first consideration must be to determine the most favourable point of view for your subject. If you want to photograph children, find out whether a squatting position does not improve matters. We speak of the bird's eye, the worm's eye view according to the observer's position, and the relationship of a subject to its background changes according to the viewpoint of the camera. Carefully note the changes in perspective often produced even by slight lateral or vertical changes of the camera position. The final fine adjustment is made with the eye behind the Leicaflex.

During close-up work, look for the most favourable position with one eye only, as this will immediately reveal disturbing lines in the fore- and background.

"Close in on your subject", "fill your film format" are the next requirements. Since you take photographs with lenses of various focal lengths it is the picture area, not the camera distance that is decisive. To improve the picture area by part-enlargement in the darkroom should be only a last resort. Basically, every picture is of course only a part of what we see. The sole question is whether this part shows the important element(s) so that it constitutes a picture. A simple means of training your eye to see such "parts" is to look through an empty slide frame. The picture area changes with the distance at which you hold the frame in front of your eye. This gives you guidance about choosing a lens of suitable focal length.

We have already mentioned the influence of illumination. The intensity of the light also has a great effect, it ranges from a blazing, sunlit day to the flame of a candle, and the question is asked again and again about suitable contrast, for modelling is produced by light and shade. The side ratio of the format, too, will occasionally play a part in composition. You can of course change this ratio to suit the proportions of your subject. Unfortunately, far too little use is made of this expedient in practice. Other means of composition are the tone values between light and dark or the delicately blended grey scale, and ascending and descending lines. You can base your pictorial effect on area or on space. There are no strict rules of composition. The play of light can produce an optically attractive pattern on the simplest objects.

The pleasure derived from photographic composition turns into a real hunter's passion once you have discovered the attraction of moving scenes. Instant reaction to surprise situations, adaptation to a continually changing scene create strong impulses and lively enthusiasm in these specialist photographers. It is not easy to capture something of the "characteristic" course of events at just the right moment. "Pictorial composition" will therefore generally be judged a little more leniently in this kind of subject.

The man behind the camera will prefer certain kinds of subject for his pictorial expression, depending on his inclination and natural talent. However, the stronger his personality, the stronger its imprint on his photographic work.

In the Louvre photography is permitted without flash and without tripod. 50mm Summicron-R, f/2.8, ¹/₃₀sec, 400 ASA/27 DIN film.

PRACTICAL TIPS

Ultra-high-speed films

Film of speeds of 400 ASA (27 DIN) and higher make it possible to take hand-held pictures at f/2 or f/2.8 in weak daylight as well as in artificial light. No supplementary light source is necessary. The advantage of this possibility is that you can capture the true atmosphere in your picture. (Although it is very often easier to use flash, if smokers are part of the picture the flash will be so strongly diffused that it gives the appearance of a curtain of fog. It is also very difficult to anticipate the effect of the light when flash is used.) The exposure meter of the Leicaflex with its high limiting sensitivity is a sure guide. If you have exposed your entire length of film in poor lighting conditions, you can mostly extend the developing time by 25 % and double the

ASA speed (add 3 to the DIN value). You will find further hints in the chapter on developing technique (p. 197).

You can manage without a tripod in a bright living room, lecture hall, museum, in fact almost everywhere. The handy table tripod will be a help should the light really be too weak; by propping the camera against a wall or a pillar you can use long exposure times without the risk of camera shake. If you have no cable release, you can use the self-timer for shutter speeds of up to 1 sec.

Family celebrations are rewarding subjects for the camera, weddings are popular. Photographs in church are particularly effective from the choir. It is mostly necessary to obtain permission on such occasions. This is easier if you give an assurance not to use flash and not to disturb the solemn ceremony.

The high speed of the film enables you, for instance in the church, to take the entry of the bride and groom. Focus beforehand (see also p. 169). A favourable distance is 14–17ft (4–5m). You are well advised to be in the church before the beginning of the ceremony so that you can choose a suitable position and determine your exposure time according to the lighting conditions. The interesting scenes outside the church can be taken on the same high-speed film, the adjustment is made very quickly with the exposure meter of the Leicaflex. There is no reason to be frightened if it indicates $1/_{500}$ sec at $f/11$ in sunlight.

With interiors in front of your camera you must remember that the depth of field is very shallow at full aperture. You will therefore try to photograph only small groups which do not make excessive demands on the depth of field. When you measure your exposure, windows or light sources should not be prominent within the measuring angle.

When you are travelling, do make a point of taking a few 20-exposure cartridges of ultra-high-speed film along. This enables you to take photographs in museums, churches, castles, etc. without tripod and flash. Sometimes photography is allowed, e. g. in the Louvre, Paris, or a small fee is charged. The shorter length of film has the advantage that you can change to outdoor subjects on medium-speed or slow film.

The dreaded graininess of ultra-high-speed films, incidentally, is not uniformly obtrusive. It is noticeable only with bright subjects and overexposure.

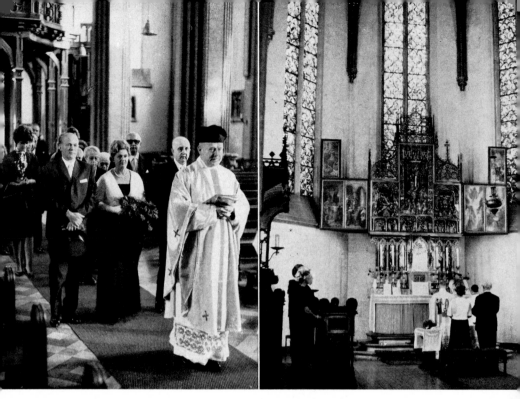

35mm Elmarit-R, f/2.8, on the left ¹/₆₀sec, on the right ¹/₃₀sec, 400 ASA/27 DIN film.

Correctly exposed pictures of very differentiated subjects show the least grain in the shadow parts. Whether grain structure becomes visible therefore depends entirely on the subject. A picture in the rain will show less grain than one in fog. The final result will also be better if you manage to fill your film format. In practice there are hardly any reserves for part-enlargement; unless, of course, you employ graininess as a pictorial medium. In this case, slight overexposure and development in Rodinal 1:50 are recommended.

Occasionally you will have to fall back on ultra-high-speed films also in sports photography, if high shutter speeds are required in unfavourable lighting conditions. They are also useful with long-focal-length lenses, because by stopping down you can obtain a better reserve of depth of field.

Another rewarding subject is street scenes in large cities at night. Here, too,

50mm Summicron-R, f/2, ¹/₅₀₀sec, 400 ASA/27 DIN film.

rain heightens the pictorial effect. You will often have permission to take photographs of ice shows, circus performances, etc., but you must not use flash. The first row of seats exactly opposite the entrance to the ring is especially favourable; exposure measurement is more precise, and there is less interference from spotlights. If you have a seat in the centre, you will try to include the entire "proceedings" in your picture. Depending on the power of the spotlights, exposure times of f/2.8–f/4 and ¹/₁₂₅–¹/₂₅₀ sec. are used. Its selective area measurement makes the Leicaflex SL particularly suitable for circus shots, because it accurately allows for the vast differences of illumination.

Over-age does not spoil ultra-high-speed films, it merely reduces their speed somewhat. Hence, if speed is essential, do not use time-expired films.

170

Document-copying film — used for a different purpose

These films have very high resolving power, finest grain, and steep gradation. But by means of suitable developers you will be able to soften the contrast and to use these films for purposes other than those for which they have been originally designed. Their performance in landscape photography is quite stunning. You will often find that thin cloud has made the sun a little hazy, and reduced the total contrast to below 1:10. Normal film would require hard paper for the enlargement of such a landscape negative; even with medium-speed films, this will quickly bring out the grain. Definition- and grain fanatics will be satisfied by the performance of document-copying film. Its only weakness is its slow speed, which is usually not even indicated on the film container, but in practice varies between 4 and 16 ASA (7 and 13 DIN) depending on the type of development. The softer you have to develop, the greater the loss of speed. A very well-tried developer is Agfa Rodinal. Document-copying films are available in orthochromatic as well as panchromatic sensitization. In combination with the yellow filter, the ortho-film renders both the greens and clouds against blue sky with pleasant luminosity. The narrow exposure latitude of films of such steep gradation will initially present difficulties. It is therefore necessary to make 3 to 4 exposures of each subject at exposure times graduated at half-stop intervals. Document films, although marketed in 36-exposure cassettes, are not stocked by every photo-dealer and should therefore be ordered in time.

Whereas the only filter suitable for orthochromatic film is the yellow filter, panchromatic document-copying film can be used with all filters up to red. For the latter, however, a tripod is indispensable; the distant features of a landscape will become very clear, but the green tones will suffer.

The quality of product photographs (jewellery, glassware, china, implements, small parts), too, is high owing to the unbelievably fine grain. An essential condition is good illumination, i. e. much light but little contrast as in colour photography for paper prints. In sum, this is an unusual material, not easy to handle, but of such extraordinary potentialities that no expert should ignore it.

People in front of the camera

This chapter does not attempt to describe how Aunt Ethel should be photographed in front of a picturesque fountain in Switzerland to give her a nice souvenir. Nor will you learn what equipment a professional photographer uses for taking a family picture, and how such a picture is taken in "common-or-garden" style. If you look for a characteristic example of medieval portraiture, you will only have to visit a picture gallery. It will mostly be half profile, the left ear visible as formerly required for passport and identity card photographs in certain countries. You can use the same lighting technique even for babies. Photograph them indoors near the window, because they will find it no discomfort there to open their large eyes. Outdoors, in bright light, their eyes usually become small and squint. Indoors, on the other hand, the one-sided illumination through the window creates too much contrast. A large, white tablecloth, at a distance of 7ft (2m) from the window and parallel to it, produces sufficient reflection. It has the advantage that by slightly adjusting the distance you can delicately balance the shadow softening. Incidentally, projection screens are far more effective reflectors than tablecloths. Although pictures taken in this way are without special effects, they represent a close likeness of the sitter.

The exposure time naturally depends on the amount of light entering through the window. Draw the curtains back completely to obtain as much light as possible. For children's portraits set up a little table with games; it is very useful to have someone to assist you in keeping the child occupied so that it behaves naturally. The camera viewpoint should never be higher than the child's head, in fact results will be better if it is a little lower. To take a dozen pictures in order to choose only the three best negatives is not a waste of film, because film is cheap; the real expense only begins at the enlarging stage. A medium-speed film is best suited for this kind of subject. Only if the background is very dark should you find out by means of a close-up exposure reading whether a shorter exposure time is not advisable.

If you want to use electronic flash during the dark season, you will find the basic principle of this lighting arrangement also very useful: light from the left or right, shadows to be softend from the opposite side by means of a projection screen.

The following type of lighting, suitable for children's portraits outdoors, is much more effective. Many of our modern houses have bright outside walls.

90mm Elmarit-R

According to the size of such walls let the children play 10—17ft (3—5m) away from them, and photograph them against the sun or with strong sunlight from the side, with the bright wall at the back softening the otherwise unmanageable contrast. When you take close-up portraits outdoors you will again find that excessively bright light from the viewing direction leads to strained expressions; you will therefore have to choose, if possible, a position in which the eye is not blinded, but without any strong top light casting shadows over the eye sockets. Unfortunately there is no hard and fast rule for such situations, because they vary so much. But usually a suitable solution will be found after some search; sometimes it will be necessary to "lead" your victim to the spot as if by accident. The desire for a photograph is not always shared by the sitter, when you will find it necessary to make all your technical preparations so that you are instantly ready for shooting.

One of the most difficult problems is raised by a good family group of more than average numbers. In the early days of photography the man behind the camera took as much trouble arranging even a large group as artistically as for instance Rembrandt did when he composed his "Night Watch". Unfortunately, nobody involved in such a procedure today has the necessary patience to do this. There are no set rules for the arrangement. Slightly diffused light or an overcast sky is generally better than sunlight. Indoor groups are highly recommended. If possible, put a 500 W or two 200 W lamps into your ceiling light. In modern rooms with bright walls and not too high ceilings this produces ideal, soft lighting. If you do not want to use a tripod, ultra-high-speed film at f/4 will enable you to make instantaneous exposures. Here, too, the exposure meter of the Leicaflex will give you good and reliable advice.

Snapshot technique

For a good snapshot technique, speed is essential. This means that you should carry your Leicaflex around the neck, and always be instantly ready to use it; lens aperture and shutter speed should be set for the prevailing lighting conditions even if no photographic subject is within sight. This leaves only one last step: that of setting the distance as soon as the situation arises. With focal lengths of 35 and 50mm you will mostly be able to guess the distance, but with longer focal lengths critical focusing will be safer. If you want to allow

Snapshot on the dunes. This trio sitting happily in the sand on the dunes are telling one another tall stories. Nothing special as far as snapshots go—until a little beetle turned up, pinching Barbara's bottom. In addition to the snapshot setting a snapshot requires also a little luck.   *Photograph by H. Gsellmann*

for the moment of surprise from the outset, measure about the same distance at a different angle according to the triangulation method (see p. 148). You will almost invariably be aided by the "photographic moment of fright", in which the situation does not change as you raise your Leicaflex to your eye. The most popular shutter speeds are $^1/_{125}$ and $^1/_{250}$ sec. It is better to put up with a larger aperture to be able to use a higher shutter speed, because an exposure spoiled by camera shake is almost beyond redemption. A snapshot is not always synonymous with a "rapid movement" shot. The most important point is that the general situation should be typical of what the photographer wishes to convey. Particularly popular among viewers is the snapshot which expresses the comical aspect of a situation. It is, accordingly, very

175

rare. Many an interesting "snapshot" is carefully prearranged — when it has ceased to be a snapshot.

Not only the Leicaflex must be ready for action; you, too, must develop an instinct for prospects of snapshots. A fairground offers more situations for the observation of human behaviour than a lonely walk; whereas you will find little to attract you in street scenes at home, you will find life and commerce in the streets of exotic countries invariably interesting. Photography is not always popular with the natives, when it will be a question of tact whether to abandon your photographic intentions or to aim with the lens stealthily, without raising the Leicaflex to the eye, and press the button.

The dynamic picture

This chapter is concerned mainly with the photography of fast movements, e.g. during sports events. The Leicaflex is particularly suitable in this field, because you can make full use of its handiness and the various focal lengths and the high speeds of its lenses.

What is a moving object? It may be a snail slowly crawling in the grass; a pedestrian doing 3 mph; or a racing car roaring along at 100 mph. What is the effect of speed on the photograph? It depends largely whether the subject moves sideways or approaches you, and on the reproduction scale — a very important point, this — at which it is photographed, because movement becomes evident as unsharpness on the film. A speed of 37 mph (60km) means a movement of almost 56ft (17m) per second. If you expose at $1/_{500}$ sec, the real movement of the object is reduced to $1^{3}/_{8}$in (3.3cm), and it should be easy to take a picture then. The real difficulty lies in finding the right moment of pressing the button. Since we react only after a certain delay, we need a certain "handicap" in order to release the shutter at just the right instant. The delay of the Leicaflex is 25 milliseconds: when the button is pressed, the mirror first has to be swung out; at the same time the aper-

During a sports event you almost invariably depend on medium to long focal lengths; the high shutter speeds permit only medium apertures, so that the depth of field is shallow. Some experience is required to assess the correct distance in advance.

176

ture is stopped down, and the shutter action proper lasts 10 milliseconds. The picture is exposed by the focal plane shutter progressively. The rational grasp of these processes is of no use in practice. What you need is a real flair for this kind os photography. It is, for instance, typical of the beginner to press the button too soon. The chapter "The way to manual skill" gives you many hints on how to acquire and improve this flair. It is also useful to make a distinction between rapid progress and rapid movement. There is no difficulty in photographing a racing car perfectly sharp at $1/250$ sec provided you follow it steadily with your camera, whereas rapid movements, e. g. during gymnastics on the horizontal bar, call for $1/2000$ sec.

Following the subject with the camera

If you follow rapid progress in your viewfinder, you automatically follow it with your camera. If you want your subject to fill the frame as much as possible, you must follow it the more rapidly the shorter the focal length of the lens you are using; the change in size of the moving subject will also be more marked. This means that longer focal lengths are better suited for this method of action shot. With a 135mm lens the object distance at a given reproduction scale is 2.7x larger than with a 50mm lens. On the other hand, the depth of field is considerably shallower with longer focal lengths. It is less well known that its effects in practice are different from what one would expect. At the same reproduction scale the depth of field is almost identical. If you focus a 50mm lens at a distance of 17ft (5m), you will obtain a depth of field from 12ft 8in to 25ft 8in (3.8 to 7.5m) at f/8, bridging a distance of 12ft 4in (3.7m). Correspondingly with a 135mm lens at f/8, focused on 45ft (13.5m), the depth of field will range from 40ft 8in to 53ft (12.2m to 15.9m) i.e. the distance will again be 12ft 4in (3.7m). Here the transition from sharp to unsharp will create an even better illusion of space because of the narrow angle of view. The longer focal lengths suffer from the disadvantage that our judgement of distances deteriorates as they increase. Here is a trick which compensates a little for this drawback.

Orient yourself when looking through the viewfinder by objects with whose dimensions you are familiar.

The characteristic phase

Let us return to our example of gymnastics photography. Analysing the various phases of movement correctly is difficult for the layman. But not every gymnastics teacher is also a photographer. Obviously, contact with such a man will be helpful. He will indicate the characteristic position by knocking.

After brief observation you will soon be able to press the button just at the right moment. In almost all kinds of sport, familiarity with the sport is as important as photographic ability if you aim at good results. Training is needed both in the sport concerned and in photography. By the way, top-class sportsmen are easier to photograph than beginners. Here is another tip: very often the stationary phase between phases of movement is particularly photogenic (high jumpers exactly above the bar, tennis players at the widest swing before hitting the ball, etc.).

It is not always possible to choose your viewpoint freely. If you cannot obtain a seat in the front row, a longer focal length and a somewhat elevated position to have an unobstructed field of view will often be useful here as on other occasions.

It is pointless to be stingy with film. If you consider the total expense of reaching the scene of activity, the cost of film is negligible. But you must think of this before, otherwise you will be left with an empty camera before the main event has even begun. It is also advisable to have sufficient fast film as reserve for dealing with the exposure difficulties of possible poor lighting conditions.

In spite of the need for making your subject fill the frame, do not forget that a few general views with the wide-angle or the standard focal length will be required to convey the right impression, and essential as a basis for orientation when the viewer comes to look at your long-focal-length shots.

CLOSE-UPS

The exciting features of the world we live in are not confined to the monumental. You do not have to go on a world cruise to receive new impressions. You can go on "journeys of discovery" just as fascinating without ever leaving an area measuring only a few square yards. Magnifier in hand you can open up a new photographic field — close-up photography. Where it begins has never been exactly defined. Many 35mm cameras can be focused no closer than 40in (1m) with the 50mm standard lens. Any distance shorter than this is classified as "close-up". Since we obtain a given object field at different distances with different focal lengths, it is not the camera distance, but the reproduction scale which is the decisive yardstick here.

What is "reproduction scale"?

The reproduction scale indicates the ratio between the dimensions of the original and those of its reproduction on the film. Our format measures 24 x 36mm; if the object measures, say, 120 x 180mm, it is reproduced, if it fills the frame, at a ratio of 1:5, i. e. reduced to $1/5$ of its original size. The reproduction scale is 1:5; it can also be expressed $1/5 = 0.2$; the decimal expression has the advantage that the exposure factor can be more easily calculated. If the ratio is 5:1, the object is reproduced on the film already at a magnification of 5 x; it measures 4.8 x 7.2mm; the photograph is classified as a macrophotograph.

The standard of reference is therefore the reproduction scale on the film, because it allows the calculation of the exposure factor. But exposure factors are significant only when a Leicaflex of the first version without through-the-lens metering is used. In the Leicaflex SL all exposure factors are automatically allowed for by the through-the-lens metering.

For the Leicaflex the calculation is very simple as long as the Elpro achromatic front lenses are used. These provide reproduction scales of up to 1:2.6 without the need for considering exposure factors.

Top: Replica of a fern leaf on a piece of rock 250 million years old. 50mm Summicron-R with Elpro VIb, reproduction scale 1:2.6, f/11, $1/4$sec, near the window, 50 ASA/18 DIN film.

Bottom: Mountings of a sporting gun, 50mm Summicron-R with Elpro VIa, reproduction scale 1:4.2, f/11, artificial light, 1sec, document-copying film.

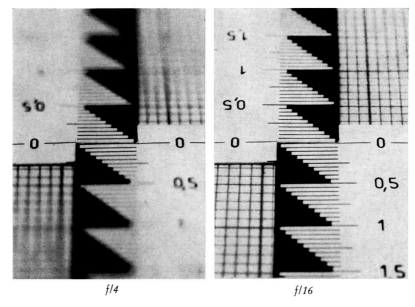

f/4	*f/16*

Subject for demonstrating the increase of the depth of field during stopping down in the close-up range. Reproduction scale 1 : 1.
The picture shows graph paper photographed at an angle of 45°, with the critically focused middle position specially indicated. Each mm on the sloping line corresponds to a difference of 0.7mm. 10mm in the picture therefore represents a depth of field of 7mm. In actual practice, the depth of field is larger than the depth-of-field tables state.

How great is the depth of field?

What are the usual lens stops in close-up photography?

When you look at a depth-of-field table you will immediately notice that the depth of field becomes shallower and shallower in the close-up range. Whereas at a reproduction scale of 1:10 at f/8 for instance the depth of field is approximately 2³/₈in (60mm), at the reproduction scale of 1:1 and the

To obtain the best possible definition and the finest grain Agfa Gevaert Agepan film was used. The film was exposed as for only 10ASA instead of the usual 40ASA (8DIN, 6DIN lower than usual). After this generous exposure a correspondingly short developing time produced a well-balanced gradation in the negative. Rodinal 1:75, 5min, 20°C.

same lens stop it will have shrunk to 0.04in (1mm). These values are derived from the table and are calculated for a circle of confusion of $^1/_{30}$mm.

In practice, do not hesitate to take pictures even if according to your table it is doubtful whether the depth of field will be sufficient. You will in any event mostly work with small and very small apertures. f/8, 11 and 16 are perfectly acceptable values, and you will often have to ask yourself whether you can afford such a small stop, or it increases the risk of camera shake to the extent of total unsharpness, even with the increased depth of field. The range of the depth of field depends only on the reproduction scale, not on the focal length, of the lens used. Since the distance from the camera subject increases with the focal length, the medium focal lengths of 90mm and 135mm are more convenient than shorter ones.

Exposure measurement of close-ups

The methods of close-up exposure measurement differ in the Leicaflex and the Leicaflex SL. In the SL close-up exposures are measured like any others. Since the measuring field is comparatively small, finding a suitable object presents no difficulties. With some close-up devices measurement has to be carried out at the working aperture; further instructions will be found enclosed with the various devices. The exposure factors arising with very close-up subjects are allowed for automatically in the Leicaflex SL. If the light intensity is insufficient when the lens is stopped down, the exposure can be measured at full aperture and the value converted for the working aperture. The situation is different with the earlier Leicaflex, where the exposure meter is situated outside the camera above the lens. The resulting parallax can be a source of error. I use the following method to obtain a correct measurement: I take a reading of a sheet of white paper instead of my object; the paper is about four times brighter than the standard object. I approach it with the exposure meter until it measures only the white area without casting a shadow on it.

Since the lens aperture plays an important part for reasons of the depth of field, I first adjust the aperture (e. g. to f/8). While looking through the viewfinder I must remember that the measuring angle of the exposure meter is slightly wider. I now rotate the shutter speed dial until the follow pointer coincides with the measuring pointer. To compensate the difference between the white paper and the real object I have to multiply the value found by 4.

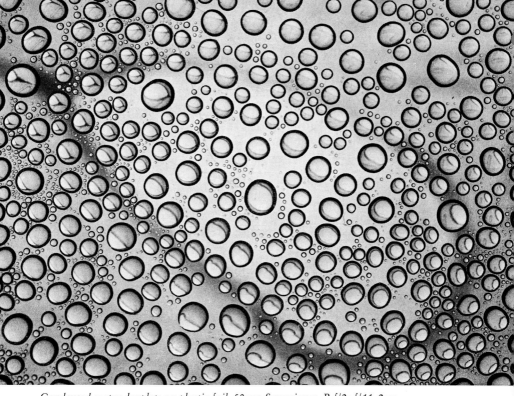

Condensed water droplets on plastic foil. 50mm Summicron-R f/2; f/11, 2sec.

In practice this is very simple, instead of $^1/_{125}$ sec I expose $^4/_{125} = {}^1/_{30}$ sec, i. e. I move two values to the left on the time scale. Naturally, measuring pointer and follow pointer no longer coincide. Exposure factors caused by extension tubes or focusing bellows must be separately allowed for.

Lighting

Where the object is small, the lighting technique plays a particularly important role. If possible, mix your general lighting with parallel light, imitating the combination of sunlight with the general sky light. The beam of a 35mm projector is eminently suitable for this purpose. But since it is an immobile source, I attach a handy mirror to its lens with a piece of wire so that I can adjust the light in any desired direction.

Do not use excessively harsh light, always balance it by means of suitable diffusion screens or fill-in devices. Always judge the lighting effect with one eye only.

Full sunlight is often too contrasty for close-up work. Whether to soften the contrast by means of reflecting screens or the light through diffusion screens you must decide on the merits of each case. Diffusion screens absorb light, whereas reflecting screens provide additional light. Mirrors and metal foils are even stronger reflectors than light cardboard. For close-up subjects in contre-jour light you can push your camera lens through a hole in the white paper. With very short distances you can hardly manage without a tripod. This is the only way to determine the picture area with the required accuracy.

Flash

Outdoor shots without sun are very successful with electronic flash, which is simple to use. The favourable synchronizing shutter speed of $1/100$ sec in the Leicaflex offers a great advantage.

You are, however, completely at liberty to increase the proportion of daylight simply by synchronizing with $1/30$ instead of $1/100$ sec.Within the close-up range even a medium-sized flash unit yields a flash more intense than sunlight, making exposures at small lens apertures possible; in the interest of depth of field, f/11 and f/16 are very useful. Difficulties of course arise because you cannot see the effect of the flash. The guide number, too, is not correct. A few series of trial exposures will soon establish the necessary correction factors; for these black-and-white film of known exposure values, comparable with those of the normally used colour film, should be used.

It is obviously simpler to carry out the test directly with colour reversal film, where processing tolerances are very narrow. The procedure is as follows: Set up an object of average brightness at a distance of 28in (70cm) from the flash lamp; arrange the reflector screen so that the path of the flash to the object via the reflector is about 40in (1m). As minimum lens aperture choose the value given by the manufacturer as the guide number for the colour film in your camera.

If the guide number is 22, start with f/22. From one exposure to the next open up your lens by half a stop until you reach f/11; note all the data and conditions on a piece of paper. The intensity of the flash is doubled if you shorten the distance between flash lamp and object to 20in (50cm); conversely it is halved if the distance is increased to 40in (1m). As the diagram shows, the flash is not mounted directly on the Leicaflex, but slightly to one side and above it. The reflector screens avert the danger of excessive contrast, and the modelling of the picture is far superior to that by purely frontal light. Any exposure factors arising in the close-up range can be compensated by a corresponding reduction of the distance between the flash lamp and the object. If daylight and flashlight are used in combination, the correct lens

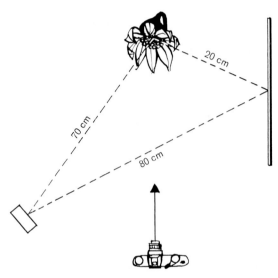

The guide number given by the manufacturer of a flash unit is not correct in the close-up range. You can determine the right aperture and the appropriate distance by means of the series of tests described in the text.

aperture and most favourable shutter speed are not easy to determine. Whereas with conventional subjects of this kind the flash serves to soften the shadows, for close-up subjects it will always be the main light source, reducing the daylight to the role of shadow softener. Determine the lens aperture according to the guide number as for interiors, and open up your lens making due allowance for the low reflection of the surrounding field, or close it if the surrounding field and daylight provide much brightness.

COPYING

We distinguish basically between two types of original:

1. Halftone originals, such as pictures, book illustrations, i. e. objects requiring a faithful reproduction;

2. Line originals, whose reproduction may be more contrasty than the original itself.

If text and illustrations are to be reproduced together, proceed as for halftone originals. Such exposures are normally made from a tripod or with a special copying outfit. To obtain parallel lines when you photograph vertically downwards you must align your Leicaflex truly perpendicularly. This is the conventional arrangement; the camera lens must be exactly above the point of intersection of the diagonals of the picture field. With the larger tripods you can meet this condition by reversing the centre column and attaching a special angle piece to it. This enables you to focus book illustrations etc. of various sizes comparatively quickly. The second condition is even illumination. For artificial light identical lamps are used from the left and right. The lamp distance should not be too short, so that the lighting angle does not exceed 45°. If it does, reflections may occur from the shiny printer's ink.

In daylight you can work near the window; to avoid reflections the distance should be about 40—60in (1m to 1.5m) depending on the height of the window. The falling off of the light across the original can be compensated by the setting up of a piece of white cardboard, which reflects the light, on the side away from the window at a certain distance from the original, which should be placed so that the slight curving almost unavoidable in books does not produce disturbing shadows.

During exposure measurement, allow for the different angles of field of the Leicaflex and the Leicaflex SL. To obtain the correct exposure time do not take a reading of your original, but of a white area. But the reading found does not yet represent the exposure time, but has first to be corrected according to the brightness of the original and the method of development. This may appear cumbersome at first sight, but has the great advantage of producing very precise values, for the accuracy of the exposure time very largely

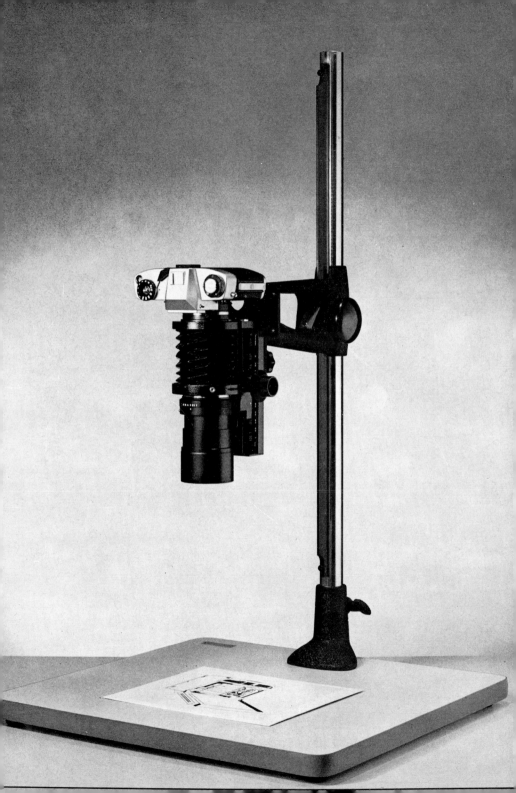

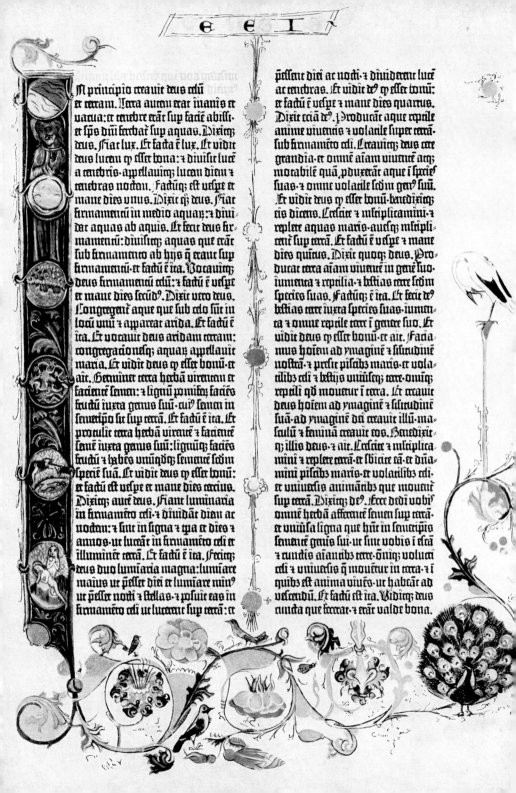

Ⓝ principio creauit deus celū
et terram. Terra autem erat inanis et
uacua: et tenebre erāt sup facie abissi.
et sp̄s dn̄i ferebat’ sup aquas. Dixitq;
deus. Fiat lux. Et facta e lux. Et uidit
deus lucem cp̄ esset bona: z diuisit luce
a tenebris. appellauitq; lucem diem z
tenebras noctem. Factūq; est uespe z
mane dies unus. Dixit cp̄ deus. Fiat
firmamentū in medio aquax z diui=
dat aquas ab aquis. Et fecit deus fir=
mamentū: diuisitq; aquas que erāt
sub firmamēto ab hijs cp̄ erāt sup
firmamentū. et factū e ita. Vocauitq;
deus firmamentū celū: z factū e uespe
et mane dies secūd9. Dixit uero deus.
Congregent’ aque que sub celo sūt in
locū unū z appareat arida. Et factū e
ita. Et uocauit deus aridam terram:
congregacionesq; aquax appellauit
maria. Et uidit deus cp̄ esset bonū· et
ait. Germinet terra herbā uirentem et
facientē semen· z lignū pomibz faciens
fructū iuxta genus suū· cui9 semen in
semetipo sit sup terrā. Et factū e ita. Et
protulit terra herbā uirentē z facientē
semē iuxta genus suū: lignūq; faciens
fructū z habēs unūqdq; sementē scdm
speciē suā. Et uidit deus cp̄ esset bonū·
et factū est uespe et mane dies tercius.
Dixitq; aute deus. Fiant luminaria
in firmamēto celi·z diuidāt diem ac
noctem: z sint in signa z tpā et dies z
annos· ut luceāt in firmamēto celi et
illuminēt terrā. Et factū e ita. Fecitq;
deus duo luminaria magna: luminare
maius ut pesset diei et luminare min9
ut pesset nocti·z stellas·z posuit eas in
firmamēto celi ut lucerēt sup terrā· et

pessent diei ac nocti· z diuiderent luce
ac tenebras. Et uidit de9 cp̄ esset bonū·
et factū e uespe z mane dies quartus.
Dixit eciā de9. Producāt aque reptile
anime uiuentis z uolatile super terrā·
sub firmamēto celi. Creauitq; deus cete
grandia· et omne aiam uiuentē atq;
morabile quā pduxerāt aque ī specie
suas· z omne uolatile scdm gen9 suū.
Et uidit deus cp̄ esset bonū· benedixitq;
eis dicens. Crescite z mltiplicamini·z
replete aquas maris· auesq; multipli=
cent’ sup terrā. Et factū e uespe z mane
dies quitus. Dixit quoq; deus. Pro=
ducat terra aiam uiuentē in genē suo·
iumenta z reptilia· z bestias terre scdm
species suas. Factūq; e ita. Et fecit de9
bestias terre iuxta species suas· iumen=
ta z omne reptile terre ī genere suo. Et
uidit deus cp̄ esset bonū· et ait. Facia=
mus hoiem ad ymagine z similitudinē
nostrā· z pſit piscibz maris· et uola=
tilibz celi z bestijs uniuerseq; terre· omniq;
reptili qd mouetur ī terra. Et creauit
deus hoiem ad ymagine z similitudinē
suā· ad ymagine dei creauit illu· ma=
sculū z feminā creauit eos. Benedixit
q; illis deus· z ait. Crescite z mltiplica=
mini z replete terrā· et ſbicite eā· z dūa=
mini piscibz maris· et uolatilibz celi·
et uniuersis animātibz que mouent’
sup terrā. Dixitq; de9. Ecce dedi uobis
omne herbā afferentē semen sup terrā·
et uniūsa ligna que hūt in semetipis
sementē genis sui· ut sint uobis ī escā·
z cunctis aiantibz terre· omniq; uolucri celi· z uniuersis cp̄ mouetur in terra· z ī
quibz est anima uiuēs· ut habeāt ad
uescendū. Et factū est ita. Viditq; deus
cuncta que fecerat· z erāt ualde bona.

Left: Reproduction of a facsimile page of one of the famous Gutenberg Bibles. 50mm Summicron,R, f/11, ¹/4sec, 50 ASA/ 18 DIN film.

Top: Reproduction of an illustration from an early book on optics by Johannes Zahn. The copying stand (16707) was used to make focusing more convenient. Here, vertical adjustment of the Leicaflex is most useful. Two desk lamps are set up at about 45° on either side to provide the illumination. 50mm Summicron-R, f/11, 1sec, document-copying film.

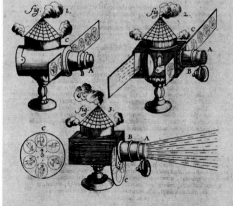

Bottom: The enlargements for the top and bottom reproductions were made from the same negative. In the first case hard paper was used, which suppressed the halftones of the background, whereas in the bottom picture all intermediate tones of the old orginal including the print on the reverse side of the page were reproduced owing to the use of soft paper.

depends on the rendering of the whites. With a line reproduction the proportion of the black lines in the total picture area is immaterial; but exposure meters do react to the bright/dark ratio.

For line reproductions, the exposure measured for white paper is on average doubled, and for halftone reproductions trebled. Adjustments are normally made by variation of the shutter speed, as it is most convenient to use f/11 for all copying work.

Among the trickiest subjects for reproduction work are dark, shiny originals such as glazed pictures or oil paintings, where reflections may occur when the photographic equipment is also illuminated. With small objects taking the photograph through a hole in a piece of black cardboard which must be slightly larger than the original (see illustration) will cure this fault. In the reproduction of coloured originals on black-and-white film, the colour sensitivity of the material and the colour of the filter play an important part. Use slow, normal black-and-white film, usually panchromatic, for halftone reproduction.

The so-called document copying films (see p. 129) are of particular importance in copying work. They are specially designed for the reproduction of ultra-fine lines and therefore have a high resolving power. Since their gradation is inherently steep, particular care is necessary in their development. Depending on the method of development they can be used either for line- or for halftone originals. Their exposure latitude is narrow, and it is absolutely essential first to determine the correct conditions by means of a series of trial exposures at graduated shutter speeds. A suitable exposure factor is 1.4, doubling the exposure time at every other exposure (e. g. 0.7-1-1.4-2-2.8 sec). With the reproduction of coloured originals the question whether to use daylight or artificial-light colour film is of importance. The Leicaflex will be loaded mostly with daylight colour film, for which illumination by direct sunlight or diffuse daylight will be suitable, whereas illumination in the shade under a blue sky will be unfavourable; reflections may occur depending on the lighting angle. To reduce this danger the original should not be placed on the ground, but mounted vertically. To ensure that the edges are parallel and that the set-up is angle-true, the lens must be level with the centre of the original. The exposure reading is again taken of a sheet of white cardboard; but the factor for outdoor exposures is as much as 4, and with

Tripod with copying arm (Schiansky). The cardboard sheet covered with a piece of black felt in front of the lens eliminates reflections.

dark originals even 5. For exposures indoors, when the exposure time increases to 1—2 sec, the factor is 6—8 (Schwarzschild Effekt). Electronic flash is a suitable light source after some practice; it also has the right colour temperature. For the close-up range its guide number must be specially determined (see p. 186). For copying, two light sources are recommended; whereas a single flash reflector can be used twice in succession at identical distances from the left and right, the use of two reflectors simultaneously is obviously more convenient since these can be connected with the synchro-contact of the Leicaflex. In the first case, the room must be almost dark, the camera shutter set at "B", and the flashes fired by hand. Note that the method of mounting the flash lamp on the camera is unsuitable owing to the danger of reflections from shiny originals. Artificial-light colour film is recommended whenever there is a frequent call for colour reproductions. Ordinary tungsten filament lamps are unsuitable because their colour temperature is too low. Photoflood lamps should be used from both sides. The angle of illumination should not exceed 45°. The factor of the exposure reading of white cardboard is 3 x for light paper with pale-coloured lines, 4 x for average and 6 x for very dark originals.

THE NEGATIVE TECHNIQUE

After the exposure the image is still latent, hidden. To make it visible it must first be developed. The developing process can be influenced strongly by the kind and duration of the development and the temperature of the developer. But results should be as uniform as possible to make photography reliable. This can be achieved only by adherence to a well-tried developer formula, constancy of, if possible, all conditions, and determination of the time with the clock and of the temperature with the thermometer instead of reliance on guesswork.

Competent photographic dealers with excellent darkroom facilities will — at least on the continent — relieve you of this work. This way out is recommended if you take photographs only rarely, or if for lack of time or space you are unable to do your own processing.

35mm negatives have to be enlarged. Although contact prints in the original size are eminently suitable for filing purposes, your pictures acquire real value only after enlargement.

Have you ever compared a picture in the conventional 7 x 10cm (enprint) album format with its 18 x 24cm (8 x 10in) enlargement? The difference is absolutely staggering. Good photographs call for a large format. Naturally, many subjects are photographed only as an "aide-memoire"; for these the 7 x 10cm (enprint) size will be quite adequate. But where pictorial impact is paramount, the effect will be enhanced as the picture size is increased.

In photography, the do-it-yourself movement is very old-established. Those with their own ideas how an enlargement should look had to rely on their own efforts from the very beginning. A darkroom of his own has for many years been the aim of every advanced amateur. It begins with a nook under the staircase where films are developed and ends with a fully fledged darkroom in a converted spare room, attic, etc. Often it is a question of available space, of facilities rather than inclination.

How to develop films is described on the following pages, because this you can do yourself even with makeshift equipment.

Films — developed by you

It is not worth while developing your own films only in order to save money — unless you are a professional photographer who exposes several films per day. But doing it yourself is great fun, and with some experience you will produce the same quality as a competent processing laboratory. By means of individual development you can match your own exposure technique even more effectively. Film, exposure, and development should be of one piece.

The following items are required for home processing:

Developing tank
developer
watch
10ml and 500ml measure
drying pegs
thermometer
fixing solution
pair of scissors
funnel
negative sleeves

and, of course, water and a darkened dust-free room.

The chemical stage of film processing consists of the developing, intermediate rinse, fixing and drying phases.

After exposure the image on the film is still latent, i. e. invisible. Only in the developer will it be blackened to form a negative. But the film remains light-sensitive even after development, because not all the silver halide in the emulsion had been exposed and blackened. Only in the fixing bath will the still light-sensitive remainder of the emulsion be removed.

An intermediate rinse must be introduced between development and fixing. Just fill the tank with water after discarding the developer, tilt it for about 10 seconds, and empty it. Pour in the fixing solution immediately afterwards. Intermediate rinse water and fixing bath should have approximately the same temperature as the developer, on no account should they be ice-cold.

An essential requirement of all darkroom work is order and cleanliness.

The various developing tanks

A developing tank consists of the light-tight vessel and the insert, which receives the film. The film is wound on the insert in complete darkness and placed in the tank, which is then closed with a light-tight lid. But liquids may be poured in and out in daylight.

Daylight developing tanks completely eliminate the need for a darkroom, as the film can be inserted in ordinary room lighting. All these tanks are comparatively simple to use, nevertheless it is a good idea to practise loading them in daylight with a length of waste film to acquire the necessary skill.

Plastic developing tanks cost less than stainless steel ones, which are, of course, unbreakable and therefore last a lifetime.

They have a further advantage: the film can be wound on the spiral insert even if this is still wet from the previous rinse. This is convenient and saves time if you want to develop several films in succession. But in this case you should immerse the film in ordinary water for about 30 seconds before development in order to compensate splashing it with droplets of water. With steel tanks, too, loading practice with waste film is recommended. At first watch the procedure, then try to do it blindfold. Round the corners of the film end with a pair of scissors before attaching it to the spiral insert; fasten the film to the core of the insert and wind it on from the centre outward. After a little practice you can do it quickly and safely.

Developer

For ultra-fast and medium-speed films a modern finegrain developer is used to advantage; it keeps the negative grain fine, does not produce excessive contrast, and at the same time has a good film speed utilization. This class of developer includes Atomal (Agfa), Fabofin (Ciba/Faber), Microdol (Kodak), Microphen (Ilford), Promicrol (May and Baker), Ultrafin (Tetenal), etc. You will find precise instructions for their use enclosed by their manufacturers.

For slow, contrasty films and document-copying films modification towards normal to soft gradation is particularly important. Rodinal diluted 1:50 has been found to be a useful special developer for this purpose. The developing

time depends on the kind of film and the desired gradation, and varies between 5 and 10 minutes.

Rodinal is diluted only shortly before use; only one film is developed in it, and the solution discarded afterwards. It is not a finegrain developer, so that its strong points can be fully utilized only in combination with inherently finegrain films.

Long-time development

On those occasions when you want to obtain the utmost speed from your films, increase the developing time and/or the temperature of the developer. But these measures increase not only the speed utilization, but also the contrast of the negative. This method has therefore only limited applications, such as reportage and sports photography in poor lighting conditions.

197

How short can the exposure be? Give half or a quarter the exposure time shown by your meter. Normal development produces underexposed negatives. Such exposures can, however, often be saved by extended development or higher developer temperatures.

Not all films respond kindly to this unusual treatment. You will mostly use ultra-fast films for poor lighting conditions. But you can force medium and slow-speed films, too, by means of long-time development. The results are often even more startling. The exposure latitude will, however, always be very narrow, which makes most accurate working essential.

Note the following points:

All exposure times must be on the short side. Normally exposed subjects will become very dense and be difficult to enlarge.

The brightness range of the subject must not be too great, as the negatives become considerably more contrasty owing to the extended or warm development. A normal to soft working developer should be used. For medium to high-speed films the following developers are suitable: Atomal, Fabonal, Promicrol and Ultrafin; for medium to slow films: Rodinal 1:100, Fabonal and Neofin blue. The developer solution must not have been used before.

At the normal temperature (20° C [68° F]) the developing time can be doubled. A higher developer temperature saves time; it may be increased to 26° C (79° F), when the developing time will correspond to that for the normal temperature. But the various films react so differently that preliminary trials should be made with a length of practice film. Note that the stop and fixing bath temperatures should be only a little below that of the developer.

Tips for development

The temperature of the developer is a decisive factor. Deviations from the standard temperature of 20° C (68° F) must be compensated by reductions or extensions of the developing time, but it is preferable to keep the developer temperature uniform at precisely 20° C (68° F). In colder or warmer rooms, place the developing tank in a large bowl filled with water at 20° C. The water temperature changes only little during the period of development.

The conventional spirit thermometer takes rather a long time to indicate the correct temperature. The measurement therefore requires patience. Mercury

198

90mm Elmarit-R. *Photograph by Prof. St. Kruckenhauser*

thermometers are quicker-acting, but not recommended as the mercury spilled in case of breakage damages all photographic materials.

Today you find making up your own developer according to a given formula generally no longer worth while. If you purchase small quantities of chemicals the price is uneconomical. The storage of large quantities is not recommended, because the differential keeping qualities of the various substances endanger the quality of the developer as a whole.

The developer solution should be free from impurities, which may later lodge on the film. Filtration of the solution is the perfect cure. For photographic purposes fairly coarse filter paper inserted in a funnel is quite adequate.

The loaded film spiral is immersed in the tank with a slight twisting movement and the tank lightly and repeatedly tapped on the table to dislodge any air bubbles from the film.

Thorough mixture of the developer solution during development is very important. Inversion tanks have been found most effective in this respect; they are inverted once every 30 seconds. In older tanks, in which the spirals can only be rotated, development in complete darkness is preferable; raise the spiral once every 30 seconds, and re-immerse it with a twist.

Darkroom timers with a bell signal have been found useful for indicating the end of the developing time. If you use an intermediate rinse instead of a stop bath, $2/3$ of the time of the rinse should be counted as developing time. The developing times given by the manufacturers should be used as guides only. The various degrees of hardness of the water may have the effect of altering these times.

Developing times of under 5 minutes are not recommended for the purpose of softening the gradation of the film. It is better to use a weaker concentration of developer and extend the developing time. Use, for instance, Rodinal 1:100 for 6 minutes instead of 1:50 for 3 minutes. After loading the film on the spiral, cut off the jagged end of film torn off the cartidge spool to avoid damage of the sensitive wet emulsion.

It is true that extended development increases the film speed utilization (see long-time development), but it has disturbing disadvantages with very contrasty subjects (contre jour, etc.), because the enlarging process becomes very difficult. After medium long development the totally exposed film end is still slightly transparent when viewed in front of a bright lampe.

It is not worth while using the developer to exhaustion. Used film developer is best poured away. If you do not use one-time developers, do not develop more than two films, in quick succession, in a tank before discarding the solution. The uniformity of the results justifies this apparent waste.

All developer solutions should be kept in full bottles since atmopheric oxygen affects the efficiency of the developer.

German law prohibits the storage of developer, fixing solution, etc. in bottles designed to contain beverages, etc. for human consumption. Other bottles, too, should always be clearly labelled.

90mm Elmarit-R, f/4, $^1/_{250}$sec.   *Photograph by Julius Behnke*

Although developers can be kept in full bottles for long periods, the date when the developer was made up should nevertheless be entered on the label. Developer solutions should be stored either in brown bottles, or in darkness.

Flexible plastic bottles are eminently suitable for storing developer solutions; when half full, they are simply squeezed before they are closed with their screw top so that only little air remains above the liquid.

Fixing

This is the third processing stage. The most popular fixing solution used today is based on the quick-acting ammonium thiosulphate available from all reputable manufacturers. Fifteen 36-exposure Leicaflex films can be treated in 1000 ml rapid fixing solution at a fixing time of 2—4 minutes or twice as long as it takes the milky emulsion to be fixed out, i. e. the film to become transparent. Thin films are fixed more quickly than thick ones, finegrain emulsions more quickly than coarse gained ones.

The advantage of rapid fixing baths consists not only in the shorter fixing time, but also in the shorter final rinse.

Once the film has entered the fixing bath, it rapidly loses its light-sensitivity. After one minute the degree of fixing can be inspected in ordinary room light without danger to the film. During fixing, too, the film must be agitated. Separate fixing solutions should be used for films and bromide paper. Rapid fixing salt is supplied in fine powder form. 125 g are dissolved in 1000ml water about 30° C (86° F). Attention: Fixing powder in the form of dust is poison to undeveloped film even in minute traces. Keep developer- and fixing solutions strictly apart. After fixing, thoroughly rinse the developing tank with water. It is better still to fix in a special vessel or a second tank. If two films have often to be processed together, the use of two tanks with two inserts becomes economical. While one film is still being fixed, development of the next can already begin.

Sculpture by Picasso, at Vallauris. 35mm Elmarit-R.   *Photograph by H. J. Bauer*

Rinsing

Rinsing the film is important. Ordinary tap water varies greatly in composition. The worst danger to your films are the tiny rust particles or grains of sand it occasionally contains. They can be removed by means of a simple cottonwool filter.

The time for rinsing the film varies between 10 and 30 minutes, the shorter times applying to thin-film emulsions. After a rapid fixing bath or a 3 % sodium sulphite bath 5—10 minutes will be adequate for rinsing. During this process the complex silver salts formed during fixing and the residual ammonium thiosulphate diffuse from the emulsion into the water. To make this process rapid and reliable, the following points should be observed:

1. Fixing solution is heavier than water, and sinks to the bottom of the vessel.
2. The flow of the water should be such that the water is renewed throughout the vessel. An outlet at the lowest point removes the water enriched with fixing salt.
3. The rinsing time is cut down considerably if it is preceded by a bath in 3 % sodium sulphite anh.
4. Complete removal of the ammonium thiosulphate salts is not possible; their concentration can only be reduced to a minimum.

In water of high lime content above 8 dH° (German degree of hardness) drying marks owing to lime residues may occur. The water can be softened by the addition of Calgon at the rate of 0.2 g Calgon per degree of hardness and 1000 ml water. This means that 4 g "photographic" Calgon (specially refined for photographic use) has to be added to 1000 ml water of 20 dH°. Information about the hardness of the water can be obtained from the local waterworks.

The washed film can either be taken through a wetting agent to avoid the formation of water droplets, or the droplets are wiped off by means of a moist piece of chamois leather. Both methods require some experience. The leather must be absolutely clean, since even a single grain of sand may lead to unpleasant results. During wiping down with chamois leather minute particles of gelatine, detached from the edge of the film, are also dangerous. But a bath in a wetting agent (e. g. Agepon 1:200) obviates the use of chamois leather. The bath should be made up with distilled water, and returned to its bottle immediately after use.

Ultra-high-speed film exposed for 800 ASA (30 DIN). Summicron-R, f/2.8, ¹/₆₀sec.

Drying

Attach a clamp to both ends of the film and hang it up to dry in a dust-free room. The bottom clamp should be weighted to keep the film taut. Avoid sun and heat from a stove. Do not inspect a film while it is wet, because the still soft layer of gelatine is easily damaged or exposed to dust. This means loss of time and tedious aftertreatment.

The thickness of the emulsion greatly affects the speed of drying. Thin-film emulsions, very popular today, dry very quickly. Only when the film is completely dry is it cut into strips of six frames each and placed in translucent negative sleeves. Rounding the edges of both film ends makes insertion in the sleeves easier. The earlier custom of keeping films in rolls is not recommended, as it easily results in scratches.

COLOUR PHOTOGRAPHY

Colour photographs can be taken with any Leicaflex. The fact that the picture is in colour is due to the properties of the exposure material, not to any special equipment in the camera. Colour photography is often simpler than its black-and-white counterpart, because the colours are not translated into grey values, but reproduced as colour scales. It is true that some points have to be watched concerning lighting and correct exposure, but especially the latter problem has lost its difficulties with the introduction of the precision exposure meter of the Leicaflex.

The colour transmission of the various lenses for the Leicaflex has been standardized to produce uniform colour rendering. Their U.V. transmission is so negligible that a U.V. absorbing filter is usually unnecessary.

How a colour picture is produced

Modern colour photography is without exception based on the three-colour method. During the exposure all the colours are split up into their appropriate proportions of the primary colours blue, green and red. Their reproduction can be either additive or subtractive.

In an *additive* colour mixture, white is obtained by the superimposition of the rays of the primary colours, blue, green and red. But this can be done only with light. — Red and green rays superimposed produce yellow, red and blue magenta, and blue and green cyan. These three mixed colours are the basis of subtractive colour reproduction.

In a *subtractive* colour mixture the starting colour is white. Dyes can be used to subtract colours. By the mixture of the basic colours yellow, cyan and magenta used here black is obtained in the region of maximum density. Subtractive colour reproduction was first introduced for colour printing.

Top: "White light" is not colourless, but represents the sum of the entire spectrum. You can easily verify this by introducing a prism into the beam, thereby dispersing the light into its spectral colours (diagrammatic representation only).

Bottom left: Additive colour mixture.

Bottom right: Subtractive colour mixture.

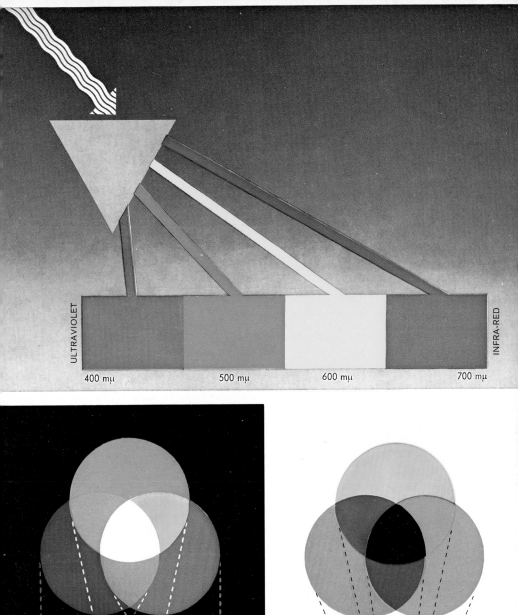

ULTRAVIOLET

400 mμ   500 mμ   600 mμ   700 mμ

INFRA-RED

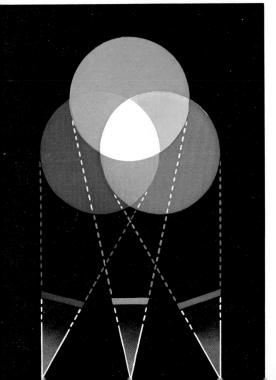

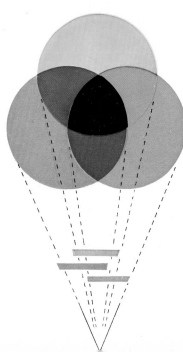

If you want to have the choice of black-and-white and colour pictures, the use of colour negative film (e.g. Agfa CN 17 Universal) is recommended. Since this film is not masked, very good black-and-white enlargements can be made of it.

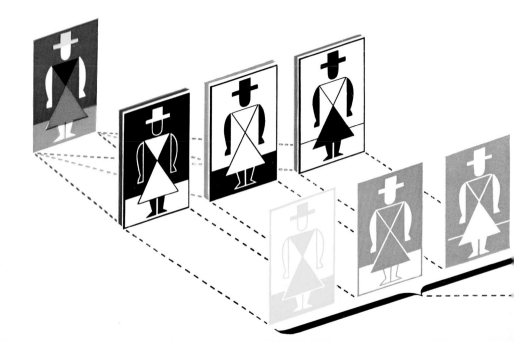

If you want mainly colour pictures, and only the occasional black-and-white enlargement, a colour negative film with an orange mask (e.g. Kodacolor X) is recommended. The mask slightly improves the colour rendering.

Structure of colour reversal film (subtractive colour reproduction

Top layer blue-sensitive	– eventually yellow	
Yellow filter layer	– eventually decolorized	
Middle layer green-sensitive	– eventually magenta	
Bottom layer red-sensitive	– eventually cyan	
Anti-halation layer	– eventually bleached	

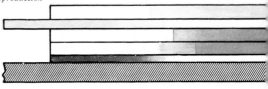

The hatched area represents the emulsion base.

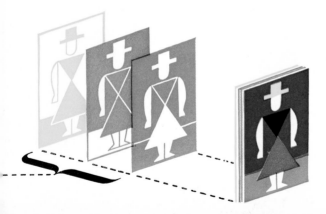

The part-images are produced in the three blue-, green-, and red-sensitive layers. Only the second development takes place in the colour-forming developer. The silver image formed at the same time is bleached out, and only the dye image remains.

Today practically all colour films work on the subtractive principle. The films have three emulsion layers on top of one another. In the top, blue-sensitive layer, a yellow image is eventually produced by means of dyes. The middle layer is green-sensitive, the dye image is magenta; it is cyan in the bottom, red-sensitive layer. A yellow filter layer between the top and middle layers prevents blue rays from affecting the green- and red-sensitive layers.

In the *colour reversal film* with colour components in the three layers, as represented e. g. by the Agfacolor reversal film, a black-and-white silver image is first developed. After a thorough rinse the film is exposed a second time, and the three different dyes are formed in the three layers simultaneously in a special colour developer. The silver image produced by the first and the second development is bleached out. This is followed by fixing and the final rinse. What remains is a pure dye image, a colour transparency of great luminosity and brilliance.

Like the colour reversal film, the *colour negative film*, too, incorporates the colour components in its three layers. But it differs from the former in that the first development is already carried out in the colour developer. This leads to a colour negative, which reproduces the natural colours only during the printing process. Some brands of colour negative film appear almost uniformly salmon coloured after processing. A "mask" had been built in for improved colour differentiation. Paper prints as well as transparencies — black-and-white and colour — can be obtained from colour negatives. The colours can be influenced during further processing, which can improve the final effect of the picture. This requires a special filter device in the enlarger. If you have no time to do your own enlarging, you can obtain reasonably-priced 2³/₄ x 4in or quarterplate enlargements from the colour printing station. They will be of good average quality, if you took care to balance your lighting. The resolving power of the colour negative film does not quite equal that of the colour reversal film.

Photograph by Günter Osterloh

Colour temperature

The term "colour temperature" occurs frequently in colour photography. It is the temperature to which a "black body" must be heated to emit light of the same colour quality as that of the light source to be measured. This temperature is expressed in Kelvin degrees °K, starting from Absolute Zero – 273° C. The higher the blue content of the light, the higher its colour temperature.

The colour temperature is thus a measure of the spectral composition of the light. In daylight as well as in artificial light considerable deviations, which affect the colour rendering, are met with. The colour temperature is measured by means of colour temperature meters. These have the important limitation of measuring only the ratio of the red to the blue proportions of the light; it is therefore possible to measure only daylight and the light of tungsten filament lamps and similar sources. Measurements of the light of gas discharge lamps, such as fluorescent lamps, mercury vapour lamps, etc. are not reliable. In any case the standard versions of these lamps are almost incapable of correct colour rendering. The following table shows the approximate colour temperatures of some light sources, and reveals the potential magnitude of the variations.

Ordinary electric light bulbs (tungsten filament)	2400–2800° K
Photopearl	3100–3200° K
Photoflood	3400° K
Clear flashbulbs	3800° K
Blue flashbulbs	5500° K
Arc lamps	4000–5000° K
Electronic flash	6000° P
Mean daylight	6000° K
Overcast sky	7000–8000° K
Sunlight (noon)	5600° K
Shadow (lit by blue sky only)	10000–15000° K

Mean daylight and sunlight have a colour temperature of about 5600° K. Our eye is able to discern the change in the colour of the light, but only if it has means of comparison. We see that the light emitted by ordinary light bulbs is too yellow when we look at a lit-up building in a twilit snowscape.

Inside the building, however, we consider a sheet of white paper "white" even by the light of the lamp. Not so the daylight colour film, which cannot be deceived; it reproduces the sheet of paper in yellow.

It would be most uneconomical to manufacture special films for the various colour temperatures. Two types of colour reversal film have been designed: for daylight (D) (T = Tageslicht), balanced for 5600° K

for artificial light (A) (K = Kunstlicht), balanced for 3200° K (Type A), and for 3400° K (Type B).

There is only one type of colour negative film, as a correction can be applied here during the printing process.

The use of filters

By means of filters divergent colour temperatures can be adapted. In actual practice it is unnecessary to use a filter for every minor change. It is true that Kodak market a very finely graduated filter set with which delicate adjustments can be made, but its use calls for an accurate measurement of the colour temperature and allowance for all other deviations resulting from the material and the exposure time (Schwarzschild Effect).

The filters normally used in black-and-white photography are, with the exception of the U.V-absorbing and the polarizing filters, unsuitable for colour photography. The *colourless Leitz U.V. a filter* has very little effect with the Leicaflex lenses, as these transmit almost no ultra-violet rays. But it is a very useful protection for the lens, especially on the beach and during sea voyages with their attendant danger of minute salt crystals lodging on the front lens surface. The filter is also more convenient to clean than a lens.

Polarizing filters, too, can be used in colour photography. The blue light from the clear sky is more or less polarized. Depending on its angle of incidence it will be possible to "darken" the sky without affecting the other colours. You will find further details about the effect and use of the polarizing filter on p.134.

Conversion filters. These are special filters permitting the use of artificial-light film in daylight or with electronic flash. These filters are salmon-coloured (Kodak 85) or brownish (Biermann and Weber K 12 or Summer K 12).

213

With other filters, e. g. Kodak 80 B, which are blue, daylight film can be made suitable for use in artificial light. In practice only working with artificial-light film in daylight is recommended. There is no loss of film speed with the filter this requires, and you will be ready to work both in daylight and artificial light. An example will serve to explain this: Kodachrome II Type A has a speed of 40 ASA (17 DIN); it is sensitized for 3400° K. With the Wratten filter 85 the speed is reduced to 25 ASA (15 DIN), which is the same as that of Kodachrome II for daylight.

Lighting contrast

Every subject shows differences, caused by the kind of illumination, not only in colour, but also in brightness. Only light and shade will make black-and-white photography effective. In colour photography, differentiation is already produced by the various colour tones. The lighting contrast should therefore not be too great. For colour transparencies the contrast range is slightly wider because it is transilluminated in projection. But in the colour paper print the brightness difference between light and shade should no exceed 1:4. You can control this by taking an exposure meter reading of a sheet of white paper placed, first, in the brightest and then in the darkest portion of the subject. The difference between the two readings represents the lighting contrast.

This has nothing to do with general brightness. A sunlit snowscape may have slight contrast. But the contrast range is influenced by the direction of the incident light which may be frontal (sun at the back), side, or back (contre jour). In the last case the lighting contrast may rise to a level where it exceeds the contrast range of the colour film. The exposure of colour reversal film is based on the bright portions of the subject. Subjects of excessive contrast can hardly be reproduced on colour paper by means of the colour negative film.

The following factors must be considered in the interest of good colour rendering:

1. Colour temperature,
2. lighting contrast,
3. exposure time.

In the mounting department for microscope objectives. Photograph by Julius Behnke

Correct exposure

The exposure meter built into the Leicaflex is specially adapted to the stringent requirements of the colour film; the colour reversal film has a much narrower exposure latitude than standard black-and-white film. A few additional points should be watched, some of which stem from the special properties of the colour film.

Colour film manufacturers enclose with their products instructions with details about sensitivity and indications of average exposure times for average subjects. You are urgently advised at the beginning to compare the results of your exposure meter with the table. Where there are considerable discrepancies check whether all the conditions were correct for exact measurement. The exposure meter is calibrated for a standard subject; for deviations see p. 36. With interior subjects the Schwarzschild Effect must not be neglected. Schwarzschild discovered that a long exposure to weak light does not produce the same density as a short exposure to correspondingly strong light. The speed of daylight colour film is adjusted to a shutter speed of $1/60$ sec. When the exposure meter indicates 1 sec, the film should be exposed for about 2 sec; when it indicates 10 sec, four times this value, 40 sec, is required. At the same time a slight colour shift occurs, which, however, differs with the material. If such long time exposures are a frequent feature of your work you are advised to obtain the relevant special details from the manufacturers of your film.

The exposure latitude of the colour reversal film varies with the subject contrast; it is thought that this amounts to $\pm 1/2$ lens stop. Every colour film is a complicated structure, a chemical work of art. It is subject to minor tolerances, which may occur in manufacture, during storage, and during reversal processing. With all the care you have taken you will be unlucky if several deviations add up. Normally they cancel each other out.

You can slightly reduce this risk by buying 5—10 films of a certain emulsion batch at a time. Test the first film, and keep the others in a plastic bag in the vegetable drawer of your refrigerator. Fresh films will certainly keep there for a year; at living room temperatures above 22° C (72° F) (normal on the continent) they will not keep as long as the expiry date printed on the film box indicates.

Blast furnace at Wetzlar.   *Photograph by Theo Kisselbach*

I use the following method for testing my films prior to a long journey: first I set the exposure meter of my Leicaflex at the appropriate ASA/DIN value, choosing an average subject with a few grey tones and a good bright/dark ratio in lateral sunlight. Using the reading of the exposure meter as a mean value I give two additional exposures each at increasing and decreasing $\frac{1}{2}$ stop intervals and make a note of these 5 exposures for future evaluation.

After the colour film has come back from the processing station I shall be familiar with its properties. I use the grey tone to assess the colour reproduction, and the transparence to determine the effective speed of the film.

Naturally, several of the 5 transparencies will be acceptable. If you lecture in a large hall, you need lighter transparencies; in the home you will prefer darker ones. These are also more suitable as originals for reproduction because of their better colour saturation.

I correct the speed setting of my Leicaflex exposure meter according to my wishes. I am, therefore, quite likely to set a colour reversal film rated at 50 ASA/18 DIN by the manufacturer at 80 ASA/20 DIN in my Leicaflex, and to expose it accordingly.

Tips for colour

Insert and remove your colour film always in the shade. Immediately set the film speed on the exposure meter.

Wrap up exposed as well as unexposed films without delay. The cartridges are not sufficiently lightproof to be left lying about openly.

Despatch exposed film to the processing station as soon as possible, especially in hot climates. Colour films left partly exposed for a long time will suffer from a recession of the latent image, and the colour balance will be upset.

Make full use of the film format; close in on your subject or eliminate superfluous features by using long-focal-length lenses.

Examine the lighting contrast. If possible, soften shadows that are too heavy. Sunlight with white clouds is better balanced than sunlight out of a blue sky.

Distant views are rewarding only when the air is very transparent. Distant views with foreground offer an improved impression of depth.

In hazy sunlight foreground subjects are preferable.

When you take a picture under leafy trees do not blame green shadows on a fault in your exposure material.

Be sparing with your colours, avoid a hotchpotch.

Fog and rain offer interesting opportunities, especially in large cities. — Use fast lenses at large apertures.

Night pictures are most successful at the last phase of dusk, when the lights of display windows and neon advertising are already switched on. Take close-up readings with your exposure meter. Standard readings do not produce a night effect, as the exposure times they indicate are too generous. There can never be complete identity of the colours of the original with those of the picture. If you succeed in producing grey areas in your film exactly as they are in the original, you will have achieved the best results your colour film will ever give you.

The processing of colour reversal film

The reversal processing of the exposed colour film requires special equipment and great care. The majority of manufacturers carry it out in their own laboratories, when the processing costs and package and return postage will already be included in the retail price. Some firms return the colour transparencies ready-mounted in cardboard or plastic frames. When you compare the prices of colour reversal films you should therefore allow for the inclusion or otherwise of the processing costs.

For films sold without reversal processing the manufacturers offer complete chemical kits with which you can process your own films. You do not save by doing this, but you will see your results earlier. The processing tolerances are very narrow. Consistent quality calls for a well-equipped darkroom with temperature control, and for the most meticulous processing.

Hints for despatch. In the United Kingdom this is done by letter post, elsewhere by sample post. For ordinary photographs this is adequate, but important material should be registered. The risk of damage is increased on the way to the processing laboratory, as the film tins may obstruct the franking machines. If you want safety for the return mail you have to enclose the excess postage for Registered Post and indicate your request.

Never put more than one film in the little despatch bag, which is designed for this number of films.

Because transparencies are shown in the light of projector lamps, do not judge their colour quality in daylight against the blue sky, but in bright tungsten filament light shining on a sheet of white paper. The lamp should be screened, and the transparency inspected in transmitted light. Transparencies should be held along the edges only.

If you are the owner of a low-voltage projector you need not mount your transparencies between glass. Mounting both between and without glass has its advantages and disadvantages. Mounting without glass imposes limitations on the size of projection, as with high-voltage lamps and prolonged projection it is impossible to obtain an image which is simultaneously sharp in the centre and in the corners. The slides curve slightly or "pop" out of focus during projection. In projection at home with a low-voltage projector considerably less heat is generated, so that the trouble described here hardly arises.

If the slides are mounted between two cover glasses they will be completely flat. But Newton's Rings will often occur; they are extremely disturbing in uniform, bright areas of the object.

They are an interference phenomenon. The layer of air between glass and film is so thin that the light cannot vibrate in all wave ranges. The disturbance is eliminated by the use of special cover glasses (Noring glasses). The fine structure of the glass surface destroys the Newton's Rings. Always make sure that the film is completely dry before glass-mounting it.

Unglazed slides are easy to store and transport. Nor can they be damaged by glass that is not completely inert. They are, however, less well protected against mechanical damage.

Mistakes in colour photography

Bright bands across the width of the film, in one or more frames at the beginning of the film:

Entry of light through the cassette mouth. May occur during film loading and unloading in bright light. A much more frequent cause is leaving the film lying about in the room for prolonged periods. Unexposed as well as exposed films should therefore always be kept in their tins.

Picture too bright as a whole:

Colours very pale, picture was over-exposed.

Picture too dark:

Underexposure. In poor lighting conditions, and in dark interiors the exposure time must be longer than indicated by the exposure meter (Schwarzschild Effect).

The whole film too dark:

This may have various causes. Film speed was set too high, the meter reading was not corrected for snow subjects. Films left partly exposed in the camera for months show a recession of the latent image in the first exposures.

The entire film black, without trace of a picture:

The film was not exposed.

Weak blue cast, especially in the shadows:

Illumination unsuitable, colour temperature too high.

Strong blue cast:

Artificial-light film was used in daylight without conversion filter.

221

Yellow and yellow-brown cast:	The picture was taken very early in the morning or very late in the evening. A similar effect is shown by daylight film exposed in artificial light.
Strong yellow or orange cast:	A yellow or orange filter for black-and-white film was used. If you work with several cameras simultaneously, mark the one loaded with colour film with a piece of coloured adhesive tape on the top.
Disturbing colour reflctions:	These are caused by large coloured areas near the camera subject but outside the picture. Bright, neutral colours such as white or light grey are particularly sensitive; thus, an outdoor portrait under a coloured sunshade may show disturbing reflections if the sunshade is excluded from the picture. Reflections from objects within the picture are, however, rarely disturbing.
Vignetting:	Wide-angle lenses at full aperture produce some falling off of the light towards the corners of the picture. In reversal film this manifests itself in a darkening of the corners. Some stopping down of the lens eliminates this vignetting effect.

222

Depth-of-field table for 21 mm lenses

Distance setting	f/4	f/8	f/16
8"	$7^3/_4 - 8^1/_4$"	$7^1/_2 - 8^1/_2$"	7 – 9"
10"	$9^3/_4 - 10^1/_4$"	$9^1/_4 - 11$"	$8^3/_4 - 12$"
12"	$11^1/_2 - 12^3/_4$	$10^3/_4 - 14$"	10 – 16"
14"	$13^1/_4 - 15$"	$12^1/_4 - 16^3/_4$"	11 – 20"
16"	$15 - 17^1/_2$"	$14 - 19^3/_4$"	12 – 25"
20"	$18 - 22^1/_2$"	16 – 26"	14 – 38"
24"	21 – 28"	19 – 34"	16" – 5'
32"	27" – 3' 4"	23" – 4' 6"	18" – 16' 4"
3' 4"	32" – 4' 6"	27" – 7'	20" – ∞
4'	37" – 5' 10"	30" – 11' 3"	22" – ∞
5'	3' 7" – 8' 5"	34" – 27' 8"	24" – ∞
8'	4' 10" – 24'	3' 6" – ∞	27" – ∞
15'	6' 8" – ∞	4' 4" – ∞	31" – ∞
∞	11' 10" – ∞	6' – ∞	37" – ∞

Distance setting (m)	f/4	f/8	f/16
0.25	0.24 – 0.26	0.23 – 0.28	0.21 – 0.31
0.3	0.28 – 0.32	0.27 – 0.34	0.25 – 0.41
0.35	0.33 – 0.38	0.31 – 0.41	0.28 – 0.50
0.4	0.37 – 0.44	0.34 – 0.48	0.30 – 0.62
0.5	0.45 – 0.56	0.41 – 0.65	0.35 – 0.94
0.6	0.53 – 0.70	0.47 – 0.84	0.39 – 1.45
0.7	0.60 – 0.84	0.53 – 1.07	0.43 – 2.36
0.8	0.67 – 1.00	0.58 – 1.34	0.46 – 4.49
1.0	0.80 – 1.34	0.67 – 2.07	0.51 – ∞
1.2	0.92 – 1.75	0.75 – 3.26	0.55 – ∞
1.5	1.08 – 2.49	0.85 – 7.70	0.60 – ∞
3.0	1.66 – 17.20	1.16 – ∞	0.73 – ∞
5.0	2.12 – ∞	1.35 – ∞	0.80 – ∞
∞	3.61 – ∞	1.84 – ∞	0.95 – ∞

Depth-of-field table for 35 mm lenses

Distance setting	f/2.8	f/4	f/8	f/16
12"	$11^4/_5 - 12^1/_5$"	$11^3/_4 - 12^1/_4$"	$11^1/_2 - 12^1/_2$"	$11 - 13^1/_4$"
14"	$13^3/_4 - 14^1/_4$"	$13^1/_2 - 14^1/_2$"	$13^1/_4 - 14^3/_4$"	$12^1/_2 - 15^3/_4$"
16"	$15^5/_8 - 16^3/_8$"	$15^1/_2 - 16^1/_2$"	$15 - 17^1/_8$"	$14^1/_8 - 18^1/_2$"
20"	$19^3/_8 - 20^5/_8$"	$19^1/_8 - 21$"	$18^3/_8 - 22$"	$17 - 24^3/_8$"
24"	$23 - 25$"	$22^3/_4 - 25^1/_2$"	$21^1/_2 - 27$"	$19^3/_4 - 31$"
28"	$26^3/_4 - 29^3/_8$"	$26^1/_4 - 30$"	$24^3/_4 - 32^1/_4$"	$22^1/_4 - 3' 2$"
32"	$30^3/_8 - 33^3/_4$"	$29^3/_4 - 34^3/_4$"	$27^3/_4 - 3' 2$"	$24^1/_2 - 3' 10$"
3' 4"	3' 1" – 3' 7"	3' – 3' 8"	$33^1/_2 - 4' 2$"	$28^3/_4 - 5' 7$"
4'	3' 8" – 4' 4"	3' 7" – 4' 7"	3' 3" – 5' 4"	$32^1/_2 - 7' 10$"
5'	4' 6" – 5' 7"	4' 4" – 5' 11"	4' – 7' 3"	3' 1" – 13' 5"
6'	5' 3" – 6' 11"	5' – 7' 5"	4' 4" – 9' 8"	3' 5" – 25'
10'	8' 2" – 12' 11"	7' 7" – 14' 9"	6' 1" – 28'	4' 5" – ∞
25'	15' 11" – 59'	13' 9" – 140'	9' 6" – ∞	6' – ∞
∞	43' – ∞	30' – ∞	15' – ∞	8' – ∞

Distance setting (m)	f/2.8	f/4	f/8	f/16
0.3	0.295 – 0.305	0.249 – 0.307	0.29 – 0.31	0.28 – 0.33
0.35	0.343 – 0.357	0.34 – 0.36	0.33 – 0.37	0.32 – 0.39
0.4	0.391 – 0.409	0.39 – 0.41	0.38 – 0.43	0.35 – 0.46
0.5	0.485 – 0.516	0.48 – 0.52	0.46 – 0.55	0.43 – 0.61
0.6	0.58 – 0.62	0.57 – 0.64	0.54 – 0.67	0.49 – 0.77
0.7	0.67 – 0.73	0.66 – 0.75	0.62 – 0.81	0.56 – 0.95
0.8	0.76 – 0.84	0.74 – 0.87	0.70 – 0.94	0.62 – 1.16
1.0	0.94 – 1.07	0.91 – 1.11	0.84 – 1.25	0.72 – 1.66
1.2	1.11 – 1.31	1.07 – 1.36	0.97 – 1.58	0.82 – 2.33
1.5	1.36 – 1.68	1,30 – 1.77	1.15 – 2.16	0.94 – 3.90
2.0	1.75 – 2.34	1.66 – 2.52	1.42 – 3.42	1.10 – 12.30
3.0	2.50 – 3.90	2.30 – 4.40	1.80 – 8.20	1.30 – ∞
10.0	5.70 – 41.00	4.80 – ∞	3.20 – ∞	1.90 – ∞
∞	13.20 – ∞	9.20 – ∞	4.60 – ∞	2.30 – ∞

Depth-of-field table for 50 mm lenses

Distance setting	f/2	f/4	f/8	f/16
20''	19³/₄ – 20¹/₄''	19¹/₂ – 20¹/₂''	19¹/₄ – 20³/₄''	18¹/₂ – 21¹/₂''
24''	23³/₄ – 24¹/₄''	23¹/₂ – 24¹/₂''	23 – 25''	22 – 26¹/₂''
28''	27⁵/₈ – 28³/₈''	27¹/₄ – 28³/₄''	26¹/₂ – 29⁵/₈''	25¹/₄ – 31¹/₂''
32''	31¹/₂ – 32¹/₂''	31 – 33''	30 – 34¹/₄''	28¹/₄ – 37''
36''	35¹/₄ – 36³/₄''	34³/₄ – 37¹/₂''	33'' – 3' 3''	31¹/₄'' – 3' 6''
3' 4''	3' 3'' – 3' 5''	3' 2'' – 3' 6''	3' 1'' – 3' 8''	34¹/₄'' – 4'
4'	3' 11'' – 4' 1''	3' 9'' – 4' 3''	3' 7'' – 4' 6''	3' 4'' – 5' 1''
5'	4' 10'' – 5' 2''	4' 8'' – 5' 4''	4' 5'' – 5' 9''	3' 11'' – 6' 10''
6'	5' 9'' – 6' 3''	5' 6'' – 6' 6''	5' 2'' – 7' 2''	4' 6'' – 9'
8'	7' 7'' – 8' 6''	7' 2'' – 9'	6' 6'' – 10' 4''	5' 6'' – 14' 8''
10'	9' 4'' – 10' 9''	8' 9'' – 11' 8''	7' 9'' – 14'	6' 5'' – 23' 7''
15'	13' 6'' – 16' 10''	12' 4'' – 19' 2''	10' 6'' – 26' 8''	8' – 125'
25'	21' – 30' 8''	18' 3'' – 40'	14' 5'' – 96'	10' 2'' – ∞
∞	133' – ∞	66' – ∞	33' – ∞	17' – ∞

Distance setting (m)	f/2	f/4	f/8	f/16
0.5	0.496 – 0.504	0.491 – 0.509	0.483 – 0.518	0.468 – 0.538
0.6	0.593 – 0.607	0.587 – 0.614	0.574 – 0.628	0.551 – 0.659
0.7	0.69 – 0.71	0.68 – 0.72	0.66 – 0.74	0.63 – 0.79
0.8	0.79 – 0.81	0.78 – 0.83	0.75 – 0.86	0.71 – 0.92
0.9	0.88 – 0.92	0.87 – 0.93	0.84 – 0.97	0.78 – 1.06
1.0	0.98 – 1.02	0.96 – 1.04	0.92 – 1.09	0.86 – 1.20
1.2	1.17 – 1.23	1.14 – 1.27	1.09 – 1.34	1.00 – 1.52
1.5	1.45 – 1.55	1.41 – 1.61	1.32 – 1.73	1.19 – 2.05
2.0	1.91 – 2.10	1.83 – 2.20	1.70 – 2.40	1.50 – 3.20
3.0	2.80 – 3.23	2.60 – 3.50	2.30 – 4.20	1.90 – 6.90
5.0	4.47 – 5.68	4.00 – 6.60	3.40 – 9.60	2.60 – 144.00
10.0	8.00 – 13.20	6.70 – 19.50	5.10 – ∞	3.40 – ∞
∞	40.60 – ∞	20.30 – ∞	10.10 – ∞	5.10 – ∞

Depth-of-field table for 90 mm lenses

Distance setting	f/2.8	f/4	f/8	f/16
28"	$27^7/_8 - 28^1/_8$"	$27^3/_4 - 28^1/_4$"	$27^1/_2 - 28^1/_2$"	27 – 29"
32"	$31^7/_8 - 32^1/_8$"	$31^3/_4 - 32^1/_4$"	$31^1/_2 - 32^1/_2$"	$31 - 33^1/_4$"
36"	$35^3/_4 - 36^1/_4$"	$35^1/_2 - 36^1/_2$"	$35^1/_4 - 36^3/_4$"	$34^1/_2 - 37^1/_2$"
3' 4"	$39^5/_8 - 40^3/_8$"	$39^1/_2 - 40^1/_2$"	39 – 41"	38 – 42"
3' 8"	$3'\,7^1/_2" - 3'\,8^1/_2$"	$3'\,7^3/_8" - 3'\,8^5/_8$"	$3'\,6^3/_4" - 3'\,9^1/_4$"	$3'\,5^1/_2" - 3'\,10^1/_2$"
4'	$3'\,11^1/_2" - 4'\,0^1/_2$"	$3'\,11^1/_4" - 4'\,0^3/_4$"	$3'\,10^1/_2" - 4'\,1^1/_2$"	$3'\,9" - 4'\,3^1/_4$"
4' 6"	$4'\,5^1/_4" - 4'\,6^3/_4$"	4' 5" – 4' 7"	4' 4" – 4' 8"	$4'\,2^1/_4" - 4'\,10^1/_4$"
5'	$4'\,11^1/_8" - 5'\,1$"	$4'\,10^3/_4" - 5'\,1^1/_4$"	$4'\,9^1/_2" - 5'\,2^1/_2$"	$4'\,7^1/_2" - 5'\,5^1/_2$"
6'	$5'\,10^3/_4" - 6'\,1^1/_4$"	5' 10" – 6' 2"	$5'\,8^1/_2" - 6'\,4$"	$5'\,5^1/_4" - 6'\,8^1/_4$"
7'	$6'\,10^1/_4" - 7'\,1^7/_8$"	$6'\,9^1/_2" - 7'\,2^1/_2$"	$6'\,7" - 7'\,5^1/_2$"	$6'\,2^3/_4" - 7'\,8$"
8'	$7'\,9^1/_2" - 8'\,2^1/_2$"	$7'\,8^1/_2" - 8'\,3^1/_2$"	$7'\,5^1/_2" - 8'\,7^1/_2$"	7' – 9' 4"
10'	9' 8" – 10' 4"	9' 7" – 10' 6"	9' 2" – 11'	8' 5" – 12' 3"
12'	11' 7" – 12' 6"	11' 4" – 12' 8"	11' – 13' 6"	9' 10" – 15' 6"
15'	14' 4" – 15' 9"	14' – 16' 2"	13' 2" – 17' 6"	11' 8" – 21'
25'	23' – 27' 4"	22' 4" – 28' 5"	20' – 33'	16' – 49'
50'	43' – 60"	40' – 66'	34' – 99'	25' – ∞
∞	285' – ∞	200' – ∞	100' – ∞	50' – ∞

Distance setting (m)	f/2.8	f/4	f/8	f/16
0.7	0.697 – 0.704	0.695 – 0.705	0.69 – 0.71	0.68 – 0.72
0.8	0.795 – 0.805	0.793 – 0.807	0.79 – 0.81	0.77 – 0.83
0.9	0.894 – 0.907	0.89 – 0.91	0.88 – 0.92	0.86 – 0.94
1.0	0.99 – 1.01	0.99 – 1.01	0.98 – 1.03	0.95 – 10.5
1.1	1.09 – 1.11	1.08 – 1.12	1.07 – 1.13	1.04 – 1.17
1.2	1.19 – 1.21	1.18 – 1.22	1.16 – 1.29	1.13 – 1.28
1.3	1.28 – 1.32	1.28 – 1.32	1.26 – 1.35	1.22 – 1.40
1.5	1.48 – 1.52	1.47 – 1.53	1.44 – 1.56	1.39 – 1.63
1.7	1.67 – 1.73	1.66 – 1.74	1.62 – 1.78	1.55 – 1.88
2.0	1.96 – 2.04	1.94 – 2.06	1.89 – 2.12	1.80 – 2.26
2.5	2.44 – 2.57	2.41 – 2.60	2.33 – 2.70	2.18 – 2.93
3.0	2.91 – 3.10	2.87 – 3.14	2.75 – 3.30	2.54 – 3.66
4.0	3.84 – 4.18	3.77 – 4.26	3.56 – 4.56	3.21 – 5.31
5.0	4.74 – 5.29	4.64 – 5.42	4.33 – 5.93	3.80 – 7.30
7.0	6.50 – 7.59	6.30 – 7.90	5.70 – 9.00	4.90 – 12.60
20.0	16.30 – 25.90	15.10 – 29.60	12.10 – 57.40	8.70 – ∞
∞	86.90 – ∞	60.80 – ∞	30.40 – ∞	15.20 – ∞

Depth-of-field table for 135 mm lenses

Distance setting	f/2.8	f/4	f/8	f/16
5'	4' 11$^2/_3$'' – 50'$^1/_3$''	4' 11$^1/_2$'' – 5' 0$^1/_2$''	4' 11'' – 5' 1''	4' 10'' – 5' 2''
6'	5' 11$^1/_2$'' – 6' 0$^1/_2$''	5' 11$^1/_4$'' – 6' 0$^3/_4$''	5' 10$^1/_2$'' – 6' 1$^1/_2$''	5' 9'' – 6' 3''
7'	6' 11$^1/_4$'' – 7' 0$^3/_4$''	6' 11'' – 7' 1''	6' 10'' – 7' 2$^1/_4$''	6' 8'' – 7' 5''
8'	7' 11'' – 8' 1''	7' 10$^1/_2$'' – 8' 1$^1/_2$''	7' 9$^1/_4$'' – 8' 3''	7' 6'' – 8' 6''
10'	9' 10$^2/_5$'' – 10' 1$^2/_3$''	9' 9$^3/_4$'' – 10' 2$^3/_8$''	9' 7$^1/_2$'' – 10' 5''	9' 3'' – 10' 10''
12'	11' 9$^2/_3$'' – 12' 2$^1/_2$''	11' 8$^2/_3$'' – 12' 3$^1/_2$''	11' 5$^1/_2$'' – 12' 7''	10' 11'' – 13' 3''
15'	14' 8$^1/_4$'' – 15' 4''	14' 6$^2/_3$'' – 15' 5$^2/_3$''	14' 1$^1/_2$'' – 16'	13' 4'' – 17' 2''
20'	19' 5$^1/_5$'' – 20' 7$^1/_5$''	19' 2'' – 20' 10''	18' 5'' – 21' 10''	17' 2'' – 24'
30'	28' 9'' – 31' 5''	28' 2'' – 32'	26' 7'' – 34' 5''	24 – 40'
50'	46' 6'' – 54'	45 – 56'	41 – 64'	35 – 89'
100'	87 – 118'	82 – 128'	70 – 178'	53 – 860'
∞	641' – ∞	449' – ∞	225' – ∞	112' – ∞

Distance setting (m)	f/2.8	f/4	f/8	f/16
1.5	1.49 – 1.51	1.49 – 1.51	1.48 – 1.53	1.45 – 1.55
1.7	1.69 – 1.71	1.68 – 1.72	1.67 – 1.73	1.64 – 1.77
2.0	1.98 – 2.02	1.98 – 2.02	1.95 – 2.05	1.91 – 2.10
2.5	2.47 – 2.53	2.46 – 2.54	2.43 – 2.58	2.36 – 2.67
3.0	2.96 – 3.04	2.94 – 3.06	2.89 – 3.12	2.79 – 3.25
4.0	3.93 – 4.08	3.90 – 4.11	3.80 – 4.22	3.60 – 4.50
5.0	4.88 – 5.12	4.84 – 5.17	4.69 – 5.36	4.40 – 5.80
7.0	6.77 – 7.25	6.70 – 7.40	6.40 – 7.70	5.90 – 8.70
10.0	9.50 – 10.50	9.30 – 10.80	8.80 – 11.60	7.80 – 13.90
20.0	18.20 – 22.20	17.50 – 23.40	15.50 – 28.10	12.70 – 47.10
50.0	39.90 – 67.00	36.70 – 78.50	29.00 – 183.20	20.40 – ∞
∞	195.40 – ∞	136.80 – ∞	68.30 – ∞	34.20 – ∞

Depth-of-field table for 180 mm lenses

Distance setting	f/2.8	f/4	f/8	f/16
7'	6' 11³/₅'' – 7' 0²/₅''	6' 11¹/₄'' – 7' 0³/₄''	6' 11'' – 7' 1''	6' 10'' – 7' 2''
8'	7' 11¹/₂'' – 8' 0¹/₂''	7' 11¹/₄'' – 8' 0³/₄''	7' 10¹/₂'' – 8' 1¹/₂''	7' 9'' – 8' 3''
10'	9' 11'' – 10' 1''	9' 10³/₄'' – 10' 1¹/₄''	9' 9¹/₂'' – 10' 2¹/₂''	9' 7'' – 10' 5''
12'	11' 10¹/₂'' – 12' 1¹/₂''	11' 10'' – 12' 2''	11' 8¹/₂'' – 12' 4''	11' 5'' – 12' 8''
15'	14' 10'' – 15' 2''	14' 9'' – 15' 3''	14' 6'' – 15' 6''	14' 1'' – 16' 1''
20'	19' 8'' – 20' 4''	19' 7'' – 20' 6''	19' 1'' – 21'	18' 4'' – 22'
25'	24' 6'' – 25' 6''	24' 4'' – 25' 9''	23' 7'' – 26' 7''	22' 4'' – 28' 4''
30'	29' 3'' – 30' 9''	29' – 31' 1''	28' – 32' 4''	26' 3'' – 35'
40'	38' 8'' – 41' 5''	38 – 42'	36' 6'' – 44' 3''	33' 7'' – 50'
50'	48 – 52'	47 – 53'	45 – 56'	40 – 66'
70'	66 – 75'	64 – 77'	60 – 84'	52 – 106'
200'	170 – 242'	160 – 266'	134 – 398'	100 – 820'
∞	1140' – ∞	798' – ∞	399' – ∞	200' – ∞

Distance setting (m)	f/2.8	f/4	f/8	f/16
2.0	1.99 – 2.01	1.99 – 2.01	1.98 – 2.02	1.95 – 2.05
1.5	2.49 – 2.51	2.48 – 2.52	2.46 – 2.54	2.42 – 2.58
3.0	2.98 – 3.02	2.97 – 3.03	2.94 – 3.06	2.88 – 3.13
3.5	3.47 – 3.53	3.46 – 3.54	3.42 3.59	3.34 – 3.68
4.5	4.45 – 4.55	4.43 4.57	4.36 – 4.65	4.23 – 4.81
6.0	5.91 – 6.10	5.87 – 6.14	5.74 – 6.28	5.51 – 6.59
8.0	7.83 – 8.18	7.76 – 8.25	7.54 – 8.52	7.13 – 9.12
10.0	9.74 – 10.28	9.63 – 10.40	9.28 – 10.84	8.66 – 11.85
12.0	11.62 – 12.40	11.46 – 12.60	10.97 – 13.30	10.10 – 14.80
15.0	14.40 – 15.70	14.20 – 15.90	13.40 – 17.00	12.10 – 19.70
20.0	18.90 – 21.20	18.50 – 21.70	17.20 – 23.80	15.20 – 29.50
50.0	43.80 – 58.30	41.50 – 62.80	35.50 – 84.50	27.60 – 275.00
∞	347.00 – ∞	243.00 – ∞	121.00 – ∞	60.80 – ∞

Index

Standard Books on Photography

Kisselbach / Windisch

The Manual of Modern Photography

204 pp. with many four-colour and black-and-white pictures, drawings, and tables.

Besides being one of the world's most successful books on photography, it is the classical textbook on this fascinating subject. It offers all the important ingredients for successful picture making from the rule of thumb for the beginner to the most cunning trick for the advanced enthusiast.

Dr. Gareis / Scheerer

Creative Colour Photography

Exposure · Darkroom · Experiments · Presentation

202 pp. All pictures in colour; many drawings and tables.

A handbook of modern colour photography with remarkable pictures and instructive text and tables. Written in a "with it" style, easy to read, full of interest, to the point yet comprehensive, and completely up to date. A book that will give any budding colour photographer the essential stimulus for creative work.

Heering-Verlag · Munich 25